# CAN WE TALK ABOUT CONSENT?

Frances Lincoln
Children's Books

Hi!

Thanks for picking up this book. It would be great if you wanted to sit down and read this.

No pressure from me, it's completely up to you, of course.

I'd really like it if you did, but honestly it's fine if you don't. I won't be offended...

...well maybe a little bit, but that's okay, isn't it?

You know, consent is a very important topic, but you really don't have to read this awesome book about it.

Everyone else is probably reading this, but then who cares about FOMO, right?

I mean, you do you, but do you really want to stop reading?

Only joking. Put it down if you want!

# WELCOME TO THIS BOOK ABOUT CONSENT

I'm Justin and I've been teaching and writing about consent for many, many years in my job as a sex and relationships educator. I've worked on consent with thousands of young people in school workshops and have written advice online that millions of young people have read, too. Together we've tackled some of the really interesting and important questions related to consent. Like...

*"How do I ask someone what they want without it being awkward?"*

*"What if I don't know what I want?"*

*"I feel like I have to please other people all the time. Do I?"*

I hope that this book will help your thinking about consent and will make it easier for you to talk to other people about it.

Although some of this book is about sex, it's **not** a sex book. That's because consent isn't just about sex. Consent is a part of our everyday lives and I think it's something that we should all be thinking about a bit more deeply. Think about the choices you've made for yourself so far today: what you've eaten, drank, worn, watched, or read. Were they your choices? Will you be watching TV later with someone, and if so, how will you decide what to watch? Has anyone asked you if you wanted to do something today? Did you respond with a "yes" or "no", or something else? Did you even really know what you wanted? Have you greeted anyone with a hug, a handshake, or a fist bump? Was that what either of you really wanted? Did you read a news story where people had their freedom restricted because of racism, sexism, or classism?

**It's a complicated topic.** It's more than just asking, or saying "yes" or "no". It's about the small stuff (what chocolate bar you want to buy) and the really, really big stuff (like your relationships). It's about how you feel about yourself, how you connect with others and how you can be part of consent in the world. And yes, some of it is about sex, but I'll let you know when we get to that bit.

**SO, HOW ARE YOU FEELING ABOUT TURNING THE PAGE?**

# WHAT IS CONSENT?

On the one hand, consent is really simple. It's wrong for people to make us do something that we don't want to do. It's also wrong for us to make someone do something that they don't want to do.

## But we should all be aiming for a much higher standard when we think about consent.

Lots of people think that consent is about asking someone else if they want to do something—asking for a "yes" or "no" answer. You know, like when people do dramatic "romantic" marriage proposals in public. Is someone really making a free choice if their only possible responses are "yes" or "no?" What if someone doesn't know how to respond but feels under pressure to say something? How can someone say "no" if they worry about hurting the other person's feelings? What if someone doesn't say "yes" or "no" at all? What if they fear the other person will break up with them if they say "no?" As you can see, consent isn't just about asking.

We're going to take a closer look at consent. By thinking about it more deeply, we can start to understand how to be more consensual with ourselves and each other in real life.

So what exactly is consent? The legal definition of consent is:

## "A person consents if [they] agree by choice, and has the freedom and capacity to make that choice."

Consent is about freedom, choices, and agreement, so it's actually a very big topic and more complicated than just a "yes" or a "no." Although it's important to remember that a "no" is always a "no," and the absence of a "no" does not mean a "yes."

We'll start by looking at our own relationship with consent. We'll learn how to find out what we need, and how to ask for what we want—even when it feels like there's so many rules we should be following. We'll think about our decision-making power, and why that's so important. We'll explore how we can choose what we want, as well as meeting other people's needs.

Then, we'll look at consent in the world. We'll cover how to ask people what they want in a consensual way, understand what "no" sounds like even when someone doesn't say it and learn how to make our interactions more consensual. We'll look at the many different ways that we might communicate with each other, and why talking about talking is so important. We'll think about how things we are taught about ourselves in the wider world can make consent more difficult.

## Consent should be happening all day, every day.

We'll look at how it's easier for some people to choose than others and why this has a lot to do with who we are, our politics, our identities, and our rights.

Consent is about choosing something to eat, what TV show or movie we want to watch, what game we're going to play, how we greet each other, and also about sex. By the end of this book, you'll be able to take more consent into the world, for yourself, and the people around you. But some of it is about pizza. I just really like pizza.

I hope that you'll enjoy this and will learn something from it. But first of all...

## DO YOU WANT TO KEEP READING?

How are you feeling about this so far? Do you want to carry on reading? Feel free to put this book back on the shelf if you're not feeling comfortable. I'm not going to be offended, okay? Honestly, I won't. **Really, it's fine.**

Let's think about this as a scale:

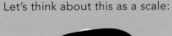

**-10**
YOU WANT TO DROP THE BOOK, RUN AWAY AND NEVER HEAR ABOUT IT AGAIN.

**0**
MEH, YOU COULD GO EITHER WAY.

**+10**
YOU WANT TO MEMORIZE EVERY SINGLE WORD.

Where are you on that scale? You don't have to decide now—you can take your time.

You could put the book down for a bit and have a think about it. Or you could have a flick through and see if this is something you want to read. Maybe you'll get more into it, or less into it. Think about how engaged you are as you read it, and remember, you can always put it down if you need to.

If you feel like you have to read it because someone bought it for you as a present, or an adult says you should read it then maybe, if you want to, show them this bit:

# YOU DO NOT HAVE TO READ THIS BOOK, OKAY?

(Sorry about the caps there. I really wanted to make a point.)

Okay, so for all the readers who would like to turn the next page, are you ready? I promise it's not the sex bit. I really will tell you when we get to that.

# CONSENT AND YOU

The first bit of the book
is all about you.

# Hi!

Why are we starting with you?
Well, as I said, consent is about making
choices and having the freedom to make
choices. So it makes sense to start with
you because it's your life and these are your
choices. This means thinking about what you
want or what you need from a choice. It's
not always easy to work out what we want
from a choice, but it's the kind of thing that
we can get better at with practice. The
more we think about what we want, the
easier it is to make good choices.

When I was asked to write this book, I decided to go for a celebratory pizza. I also thought that talking about pizza would be a good starting point for talking about consent. So this next bit is all going to be about pizza. **A lot.**

At this point, I should say if pizza isn't your thing, that's okay. You can take this example and apply it to anything: a chocolate bar, a can of soda, what to watch on TV, or a game you might play. The pizza here is an analogy.

You might be able to think of other examples like this in your life. What if someone said you can watch TV, but only if you can watch the same thing that you watch over and over again? Or if you can only play soccer, but you can play in goal? Or that you can get your hair dyed, but it has to be blue? We need more than one option to be the one we can really choose, than to have these examples so these examples don't allow much room for **real consent.**

When there is only one thing that we can eat at a pizza place, our choice becomes: do you want to eat, or do you not want to eat? That's not a choice. In fact, it's barely a choice at all. **If consent is about choices and freedom, then it's more than just avoiding something we don't want.** Not much choice or no consent at all.

# Chapter One
# I went for a pizza

Anyway, back to pizza. At my local pizza place, they have a menu of five things. It's one of those places where they don't give you much choice because for a pizza to be a real "authentic pizza" it can only be made from a few ingredients. For example, they wouldn't let you have pineapple on your pizza because that's not **"real"** pizza.

This idea of real pizza, or "proper pizza," means that I have less choice. It's a **"Should Story"**, and that will keep coming up in the book. A Should Story is told to us to try to make us do what is considered "normal," even if it's not harmful to do otherwise. Other examples of Should Stories are, "you must wear matching socks," or "you can't eat sweet things before savory," or "when you're listening to music in your ear buds you shouldn't lip sync along in public."

I questioned Choosing my pizza. Was I following the situation I was in. Making a choice to try and "fit in?" (I was just for me, or was I wearing a Should Story, or was I didn't have dessert and This pressure to fit in really reduces our choices and Making choices in life. on other people's opinions isn't really consent at all.

On the menu, two of the choices were too boring for me (tomato, or cheese and tomato) and another had mushrooms on (I'm allergic), so I could just choose between two pizzas: anchovy or salami). If I was a vegetarian, I would have had the choice of three pizzas and two of them were quite dull. If I was a vegan, I would only have been able to choose one very boring pizza.

# INFINITY

If I were to open up a pizza place that was all about consent and loads of choices, I'd call it

## INFINITY PIZZA™

and I'd do things differently.

I'd have **regular wheat base, but also gluten-free bases** for my gluten-intolerant friends.

These two different bases could be made in several different styles:

thin and crispy
thick and doughy
somewhere in between.

I'd have different styles, like:
### ITALIAN

Neapolitan   Roman   Sicilian

### AMERICAN

CHICAGO   New York   DETROIT   and yes, even a HAWAIIAN.

 I'd have a **TURKISH** pizza called "pide," which is thin and crispy.

And **ETHIOPIAN** pizza.

 I'd have **FLAMMKUCHEN**.

 There'd be **ROTI** pizzas.

 And even Japanese pizza bases.

They would be rectangular or round. You can't have triangles, though. Sorry, but no—I draw the line at triangles.

I'd also have all the **TOPPINGS** you'd expect at a pizza place...

cheeses   olives   peppers   onions

That's a lot of choice, right? Wait til you see the **DESSERT** menu!

Only joking, it's just . . .

# PIZZA™

I'd have different **SAUCES**

classic tomato sauce

garlic oil

barbecue sauce

cream cheese

sour cream

Or, shockingly, there'd be the option to have no sauce at all! I know—**scandalous.**

eggplant

pineapple (you do you)

mushrooms (no, thanks)

But then I'd have other things, like...

Brussels sprouts

strawberries (hey, I'm not here to judge)

TIRAMISU

But back to the main course. What pizza would you choose? Infinity Pizza™ has so many choices—does that make your choice easier or harder to make? Would your brain melt if you had that much choice, or would you be excited to make the best pizza anyone has ever had? It would take me a long time to choose, so I'd rather just stick with my local pizza place and order from the two pizzas I know I like.

It's hard to have the pizza we want when we don't get very much choice. But it can also be really hard to have so many options when we don't know what we might like, or what might go well together. It's also hard to know whether we are ordering a pizza that we think is "normal," like what everyone else orders, or whether we are doing something just for us. The Should Story about pizza tells us that having a square pizza with barbecue sauce, cheese, and strawberries is not a normal pizza, even if we really like that. So we need to start being able to

# LISTEN TO OURSELVES MORE.

That's what we're going to look at now.

## HOW TO CHOOSE THE PIZZA YOU ACTUALLY WANT

Okay, so maybe Infinity Pizza™ might not be a great idea because it has too many choices and not enough ideas about what might be good. Many really popular pizza places offer lots of choice without having to go as far as Infinity Pizza™. They offer lots of set pizzas with different names, such as margherita, napolitana, quattro stagioni, americana, and fiorentine.

But they also offer different toppings so that you can adapt one of their set pizzas to suit your tastes. They make suggestions of what toppings would go well on a pizza for you to choose from. Or you can choose to substitute other toppings. It's clever because they are giving you a choice of how much you want to choose. You can choose to choose or they can help choose for you.

Another example of this is when you're watching something online and you get recommendations about what you might like to watch next. These recommendations are sometimes based on the things that you like to watch (sneaky, clever internet). You can choose to watch anything you want from millions and millions of clips, or you can choose not to choose and let the internet tell you what to watch.

At Infinity Pizza™, I could train the waiters to help you choose. They could ask questions such as: is there anything that you can't or won't eat? How hungry are you? Do you like sweet, sour, bitter, salty, or savory tastes? Do you like spicy or cool flavors? Are you in the mood for something adventurous or something familiar? The waiters would take their time and encourage you to slow down and listen to what your body is telling you. These are the kinds of questions we could learn to ask ourselves, and learn to give ourselves time to answer them.

Think of the times when you've chosen a pizza (or anything else) and regretted your choice. It's so hard for us to really listen to our body and say, "I want that one." Often that's because we are feeling rushed and not taking the time to really listen to our wants and desires. Or maybe we are continually being distracted by all the Should Stories that we are constantly being told, rather than what we actually want. Maybe sometimes we just don't take the time to listen to what we want, because we don't think we deserve to have what we really want.

So there's my local pizza place with the Should Story and not much choice. Then there's Infinity Pizza™, which has too much choice and not enough guidance on how we can choose. And there's the middle-ground pizza place where, with help from the people making us the pizza, we might be able to listen to our body about what we actually want.

## WHY I'M OVERCOMPLICATING PIZZA

There's a reason behind why I'm going into pizza in such great detail. It's important, okay? Every day we make choices, like what shows to watch, what chocolate or pizza to eat, or what soda to have. But sometimes, our choices are really big ones, such as: do I want to be friends with this person? What classes should I take at school? Do I want to have sex?

So, learning to choose, even about the small things, is an important practice. The more we practice, the better we'll get and the quicker we'll be at making choices for ourselves.

If we do that on a regular basis, then we can increase our ability to choose things. There's a word that academics use for this: agency.

I WENT FOR A PIZZA

# Chapter Two
# Agency
## (clout, or ooooompf)

Agency is about actively and intentionally doing things.

Making things happen. Making choices and the power to make choices. Asking for things. Exerting our freedom. Seeking out what we want in life. Trying to make our lives good and also trying to do this for other people. Living our best life. Us doing us. That kind of thing. You know, big and important stuff. When you hear agency, think power, "clout," or "ooooompf."

If we aren't actively choosing things or not making things happen, then we aren't acting with agency. It's harder to see ourselves as having freedom if we aren't actively making choices. So picking the pizza (or the chocolate bar, soda, or TV show) that we want is actually about living and having a sense of our own power to act.

## The more we do it, the more we get to have it.

However, there are always going to be restrictions. We can't always do whatever we want—the world just wouldn't function if we did. It's not possible to separate ourselves off from the rest of the world. Like you can't break the law, and I'm not telling you that you should listen to your parents... but maybe I am a little bit.

We also shouldn't do things that restrict other people's agency. The choices that we make about our own lives shouldn't limit the

choices that other people have over theirs. We'll look at this when we get to the Consent and Others section. And just as we might do things that affect someone else's agency, the reverse is also true.

Sometimes it's not just another person but a group of people, the government, big companies, or cultures and traditions that restrict how much agency we have. And as we've seen already, Should Stories can restrict how much agency we have. But imagine a world where

everyone was able to do what they wanted without hurting anyone else. In fact, imagine a world where not only were people not hurting others with their choices, they were helping as many people as possible make their own choices too. Everyone being freed to do whatever they wanted without hurting others or themselves would be wonderful. A world in which everyone tries to maximize each other's agency.

## IT'S NOT THE SAME FOR EVERYONE

The idea of actively making choices about our lives might sound a bit obvious to some of you reading this (Hi). But for some of you it might be quite a new or strange idea (Hi to you, too). Some people have more capacity to choose what they want to do than others and so they have more agency. As we'll see later, the discrimination that people face based on their gender, race, sexuality, class, or ability means that some people have more power (or privilege) than others. We'll cover this in more detail in chapter 10, but for now it's important to understand how we can all learn to nurture our agency and why this is important.

Some of us will find it easier to choose our pizzas because we have enough money to eat pizza a lot. So it doesn't really matter if we choose one we don't like because there's always more pizza. However, some of us will find it less easy to choose because we don't have enough money to eat pizza a lot, so we might not know what we do and don't like yet.

Some people might not be able to get into the pizza place because they don't have good disabled access. Maybe people of color might be treated worse if the

boss of the pizza place is racist. A straight couple might feel like they could hold hands in the restaurant, but a same-gender couple might not feel able to. Agency is not something that is shared out fairly in society. People with less money have fewer choices over what they spend and so have to be more careful with their choices than people with more money. Disabled people have fewer choices over where they can go because many places are just not accessible enough. Same-gender couples often find it difficult to display affection publicly because of homophobia or biphobia. Racism means that people of color might be less safe or have fewer rights in various parts of the world. Sexism means that many women don't get treated as well as men at work and also usually get paid less. Transphobia means that many trans people find that they are less able to wear what they want because other people may hurt them. This is important stuff and we'll come back to this later on.

Having said all of this, agency is something that we can learn to grow where we can. And learning to do this through simple everyday things (like pizza, chocolate, TV shows, and soda) is really important. Learning to grow our agency is important to help us experience joy, excitement, and comfort, but it's also important for other reasons.

Warning: I'm about to bring the mood down.

# WHY AGENCY IS IMPORTANT

Sometimes, although we have agency, we have no choice over something happening to us. It could be something like:

**Someone we care about dying: a family member; a friend; a pet; a famous person we felt connected to**

**A relationship ending**

**Illness or injury**

**Being hurt by someone**

**Something else that might cause physical or emotional pain and injury**

When someone does something to us rather than with us, or something happens without our consent, it's called non-consensual. That's because we don't have a choice. We'll talk more about this later and I'll give you a heads up when we do.

The antidote to crappy things that can happen to us is more agency and that means more consent. More choices and more freedom for ourselves can't always protect us from bad things happening to us, but they can remind us of who we are and of our power to act, even when choices are taken from us.

Thinking carefully about your own choices and what will be best for you is really, really important, even when you're feeling pretty okay with life. But it's especially important when you're not feeling so okay, or if you've had some of your agency taken away. Learning to practice self-consent, or self-care, is an extremely good idea.

**"What is self-care?" I hear you ask.**

In a nutshell… Self-care isn't about eating a chocolate bar, having a bubble bath, or doing some exercise. It's about choosing to do something for yourself. It's the process of choosing which chocolate bar you will have, and noticing how it tastes. Self-care is about deciding how bubbly your bubble bath is, whether or not to play music, or if you want to have your rubber duck with you. It's also about noticing what kind of exercise or movement might be useful to you, listening to your body, and gently giving

it what it needs. To do this, you could practice listening to your body when you are making a decision about what to do. What does it feel like in your body when you are joyful, sad, scared, or excited about something? Can you learn to notice the feelings in your body and where they start from? This isn't easy to do and you won't always get it right every time— I know that I don't. But trying to do it is a really good thing to practice. It's not what you do, but the process of how you do it.

**That's what self-care is.**

So we started with you. Now, how do you do all of these things with other people?

# CONSENT
# AND
# OTHERS

Learning how to treat ourselves consensually is really important, but learning to do it while also treating someone else consensually is the hard bit. So in this, the biggest section of the book, we'll look at how to negotiate what we do with other people. We'll think about how to meet someone else's needs as well as our own. We'll learn how to ask for things, and how to hear and say "no." We'll explore how to do more consensual greetings with each other (hugs, handshakes, or fist bumps). Then we'll get onto the sex bit and learn how to put consent into practice when having sex, if sex is something you might want to do at some point in your life. Lastly, we'll think about how we can choose which movie to see with a group of friends—that's group consent!

## Chapter Three

# Doing things with other people

By now, you should have a pretty good idea of how we can try to do consent with ourselves and why that's important.

In this bit, we're going to look at how you can do consent with others.

Whenever you are doing something with someone else, it's important to try to make it consensual for both people involved. In other words, you both freely agree and choose something that you both want to do. Doing something that you want to do is important, as we discussed in the last chapter. But you shouldn't make someone else do something that you want to do just because you want to do it. Just as someone else shouldn't do that to you.

Consent with another person is more difficult because often you'll have to make some kind of compromise. Even if you are really trying to give each other as much agency as possible, you might not be able to make a choice that is absolutely ideal for you (even if you freely agree to do it). So you might end up sharing a bit of a dull pizza, watching a show you've seen before, or playing a game that you are a bit bored of.

Sometimes people prefer to do things by themselves, just to avoid compromising with someone else. That's fair and I think that sometimes it is better just to do things by yourself. It's certainly better to do that than to make someone else do what you want, if they don't want to. However, if you avoid doing things with other people, you'll miss out. Going through the process of talking about what you need and finding ways to meet each other's needs is the key to really good relationships with people.

Having someone else trying to meet your needs while also trying to meet their own is a lovely thing. When you do this, you are also creating a lot of agency for you both: fun times, shared memories, and support. These are moments you couldn't have captured on your own and that could only have been shared together. This is what forms wonderful and loving relationships. By putting consent at the heart of your relationships, you can both enjoy doing things together more than you might if you'd done something by yourself.

Talking about this stuff can be hard work and a bit frustrating at times. Maybe you've experienced this yourself? This chapter is all about trying to make it a little easier, and there are lots of ideas about how you could do it. Once you've learned some of these ideas and put them into practice in your everyday life, it will get easier.

# HOW TO MEET EACH OTHER'S PIZZA NEEDS

Before we go any further, let's have another quick example of how people can meet each other's needs when they share a pizza. If you're bored of me talking about pizza, you could imagine choosing a movie to watch together.

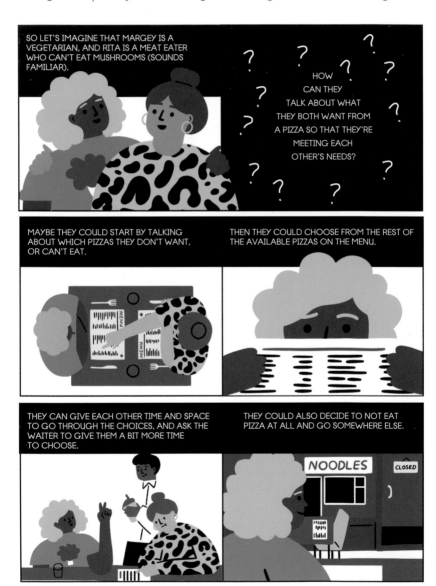

IF THEY WERE CHOOSING A MOVIE...

THEY COULD TALK ABOUT WHAT KIND OF SHOW THEY FEEL IN THE MOOD FOR. A COMEDY, A DRAMA, A THRILLER, OR A PIZZA-THEMED ACTION MOVIE.

THEY COULD SAY WHICH SHOWS THEY DON'T WANT TO WATCH OR IF THEY HAVE ANY PHOBIAS. THEY COULD SAY IF THEY DON'T LIKE *2 THIN, 2 CRISPY*, AN ACTION FILM ABOUT A PIZZA CHEF SLASH CRIME-FIGHTING HERO.

THEY COULD GIVE EACH OTHER TIME TO DECIDE WHAT THEY'D LIKE TO WATCH.

PERHAPS IT'S SOMETHING ROUND THAT'S COOKED IN AN OVEN COMING TOWARD THEM.

BUT BACK TO THE RESTAURANT...

IF THEY DO DECIDE TO STAY AT THE PIZZA PLACE, WHAT COULD THEY DO TO INCREASE THEIR PIZZA JOY?

ARE THERE OTHER TOPPINGS THAT THEY COULD CHOOSE THAT WOULD MAKE THEM BOTH HAPPY?

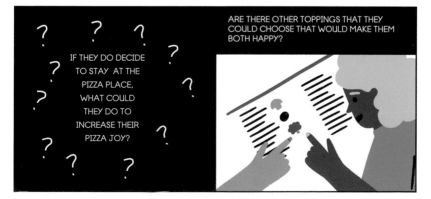

COULD THEY DIVIDE THE PIZZA IN TWO SO THAT MARGEY HAS MUSHROOMS ON HER SIDE AND RITA HAS PEPPERONI ON HER SIDE?

MAYBE THEY COULD ADD SOME EXTRA TOPPINGS.

PERHAPS RITA IS HAPPY NOT HAVING ANY MEAT ON A PIZZA THIS TIME BECAUSE THEY KNOW MARGEY DOESN'T LIKE TO SMELL IT.

PERHAPS THEY CAN ENCOURAGE EACH OTHER TO AGREE ON WHAT THEY BOTH WANT ON THE PIZZA RATHER THAN HAVING WHAT THEY THINK THEY SHOULD HAVE.

THEY COULD MAXIMIZE THEIR PLEASURE IN EATING THE PIZZA BY BEING SLOW, NOTICING HOW IT TASTES, AND TELLING EACH OTHER ABOUT HOW GOOD IT IS.

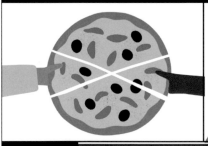

AT THE END, THEY COULD TALK ABOUT THEIR THOUGHTS ON THE PIZZA AND WHAT THEY MIGHT DO DIFFERENTLY NEXT TIME.

DURING WHATEVER THEY ARE WATCHING, THEY COULD NOTICE WHETHER THEY ARE ENJOYING IT AND ASK EACH OTHER WHAT THEY THINK ABOUT IT.

MAYBE THEY COULD AGREE TO WATCH IT FOR THE FIRST PART AND THEN SEE IF THEY WANT TO CARRY ON AFTER THAT IF ONE PERSON IS REALLY INTO IT.

OR MAYBE ONE PERSON COULD JUST PLAY ON THEIR PHONE WHILE THE OTHER PERSON WATCHES WHAT THEY WANT TO WATCH.

THE END.

I THINK THAT BY THE END OF IT, EVEN IF NEITHER OF THEM GOT THEIR PREFERRED PIZZA OR MOVIE, THEY WOULD HAVE BOTH REALLY ENJOYED IT. THE PROCESS OF TRYING TO MEET EACH OTHER'S NEEDS WILL PROBABLY ALSO MAKE THEM FEEL CLOSER AND MORE TRUSTING OF EACH OTHER. IT'S THE PROCESS OF TRYING TO MAKE SOMETHING AS CONSENSUAL AS POSSIBLE THAT IS THE KEY TO GOOD RELATIONSHIPS. IT'S NOT WHAT YOU DO, IT'S HOW YOU DO IT TOGETHER. NOW WE'RE GOING TO LOOK AT HOW TO ASK AND HOW TO HEAR A "NO."

Chapter Four

# How to ask

An important part of consent is learning how to ask.

It's really not cool to do something to someone without asking them first. That's pretty basic bad behavior and we should never do it. However, we can also ask people to do things in ways that aren't consensual without meaning to. If you're confused about how to ask for consent, over the next few pages are some things to help you understand it a bit more.

## DO THEY WANT YOU TO ASK?

Obviously you won't know if you don't ask, but has the person given you an indication that they'd be interested in you asking them for something? For example, if you were going to ask someone out on a date, have they shown any interest in you or in going on a date with you? It's usually not a good idea to ask someone to do anything out of the blue. It makes it more likely that they will say no and so more likely you might feel a bit stung by rejection.

## MAKE IT CLEAR WHAT YOU ARE ASKING FOR

If you are asking someone to make a choice, then it's best to tell them as much as you can about what you are asking for and why. So if you are asking someone to go on a date with you, is that because you would like to kiss them, because you want to get to know them, or so you can be friends? It wouldn't be very consensual if you suggested doing something without telling them everything it might involve. This doesn't mean you need to use the words, "Want to go on a date so we can kiss?" Instead, you can give the other person an idea of what it is that you want from the thing that you are asking for. Like is this a friend date, or a romantic date?

## WHO ARE YOU ASKING FOR?

A classic mistake that people make when asking someone to do something is that they don't make it clear who it's for. Is it something you want them to do for you, for you to do for them, or for you to do together? I think it would be great if we could all be a bit clearer about this. It's okay for us to ask someone to do something for us and it's okay for us to do something for someone else because someone has asked.

For example, if someone close to you looks like they might want a hug, you could ask them if that was something that you could do for them. If you were the one wanting a hug, it's better for you to ask them if they could hug you. However, if you asked them if they wanted a hug, when it was actually you who wanted the hug, then you've made this about your needs and wants while pretending that it was about theirs. That's not okay. If you want a hug, you could ask for a hug.

## ASK IN A WAY THAT GIVES OPTIONS

Remember that consent is all about agency. So how can you ask in a way that gives the person the most amount of choice possible? A good starting point here is to ask a question that gives more than two options. So instead of, "Do you want to watch *2 Thin, 2 Crispy* later?", you could

say, "What are your thoughts about watching something like *2 Thin, 2 Crispy* later?" If we were asking someone for a hug, we could say, "What are your thoughts about having a hug?" or "How do you feel about a quick hug, a cuddle, or me putting my hand on your shoulder?" Even better, we could say, "Is there any kind of support that you might like right now? Like a hug, a bar of chocolate, some advice, or some space?"

We need to get better at asking people so that they have options. If the options we give someone are, "Do you want this, or do you not want this?", that doesn't really give them much freedom. So even though it can be awkward, start thinking about how you can ask for something in a way that gives the person more than just the choice of doing it or not doing it. Aim for at least three possible choices of doing something, as well as just not doing anything. It's not always easy, but it's what we should aim for, I think.

## JUST ASK ONCE

Once you've asked them, that's it—
only ask them once. You can ask if they
have any other questions, or if they
need any other information that might
help them come to their decision, but
once they have all of that, give them
space. It's not consensual to try to
make someone do what you want them
to do. Don't pester or nag someone
into doing something. Be polite
and say please if you want to, but don't
say "Pleeeeeeeeeeeeeeeeeeease"
or "I beg of you."

## GIVE THEM TIME AND SPACE

Give them the room to be able to come to their decision. Don't just stand there and wait until they say yes or not. Have you ever seen a public marriage proposal on TV or social media? I watch those things through my hands, cringing with embarrassment. This situation is extremely bad for a number of reasons: she's under pressure to answer the question then and there; she only has a choice of "yes" or "no;" everyone else around her is pressuring her to say "yes," because that's what women are supposed to do. (You might notice that I've used the pronouns she/her here. That's because it's usually a man asking a woman—we'll talk about Should Stories for women later.)

## LISTEN TO THEIR NO

Ideally we'd ask questions that don't need "yes" or "no" answers. But if someone does say "no" to you, then you should listen, accept their decision, and not try to change their mind. Saying "Oh, go on...," or "You know you want to!" or "Can't you do this one thing for me?" or "If you loved me, you would," is not asking consensually. These are ways of trying to make the other person do something out of guilt, or by making them feel like they owe you something. It's ignoring their agency and, as we've discussed before, that's not cool. Stop it.

Chapter Five

About

N

Sadly, some people are going to put us in a position where we have to say "no" sometimes.

We shouldn't be put in these situations in the first place and shouldn't need to say "no". But because this does happen, I think it can be useful to learn how to say "no" in these sorts of situations. If we are being asked to do something consensually, then we would be able to choose different things based on what we may or may not want to do. If we are having to say "no," it's because we haven't been given enough choices.

## OUR ACTIONS MEAN NO TOO

We don't just say "no" with words—we say it with our actions. In fact, research shows that people don't often use the word "no" when they are being asked whether they want to do something. Think about the times when you didn't want to do something. Instead of saying "no," you might have said "Ummmmm" or "I dunno" or went quiet and shrugged your shoulders. These are all forms of "no", and hopefully the other person would have understood that. In fact, the same research found that we understand that different gestures or phrases mean "no," even if someone doesn't say "no."

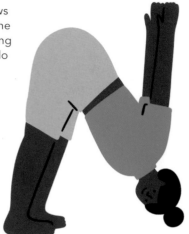

Most people can recognize when someone is saying "no" with their body rather than with their mouths. However, there are good reasons why many people can't recognize this kind of unspoken "no." We have different levels of understanding of other people's reactions. Some of us have difficulty reading people. If this applies to you, you might need to talk with the person you're asking about what their response is (and perhaps explain that you find it difficult to understand body language).

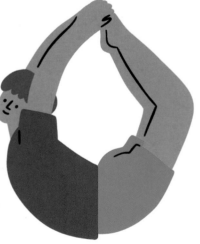

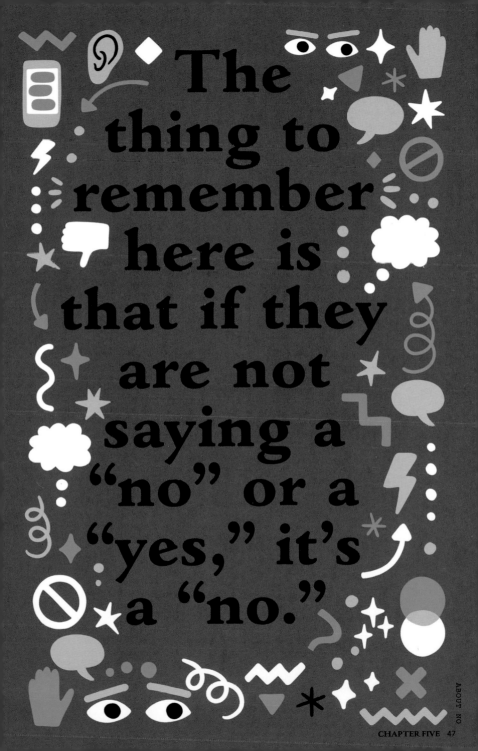

The thing to remember here is that if they are not saying a "no" or a "yes," it's a "no."

$\varnothing(NO) \neq YES$

$2 + 2 =$

$\Sigma$

N Y

Ṅ

4

# AN ABSENCE OF A

$(\frac{1}{2} \times$

$\pi$

0%

$n \neq y$

NO

N

Y

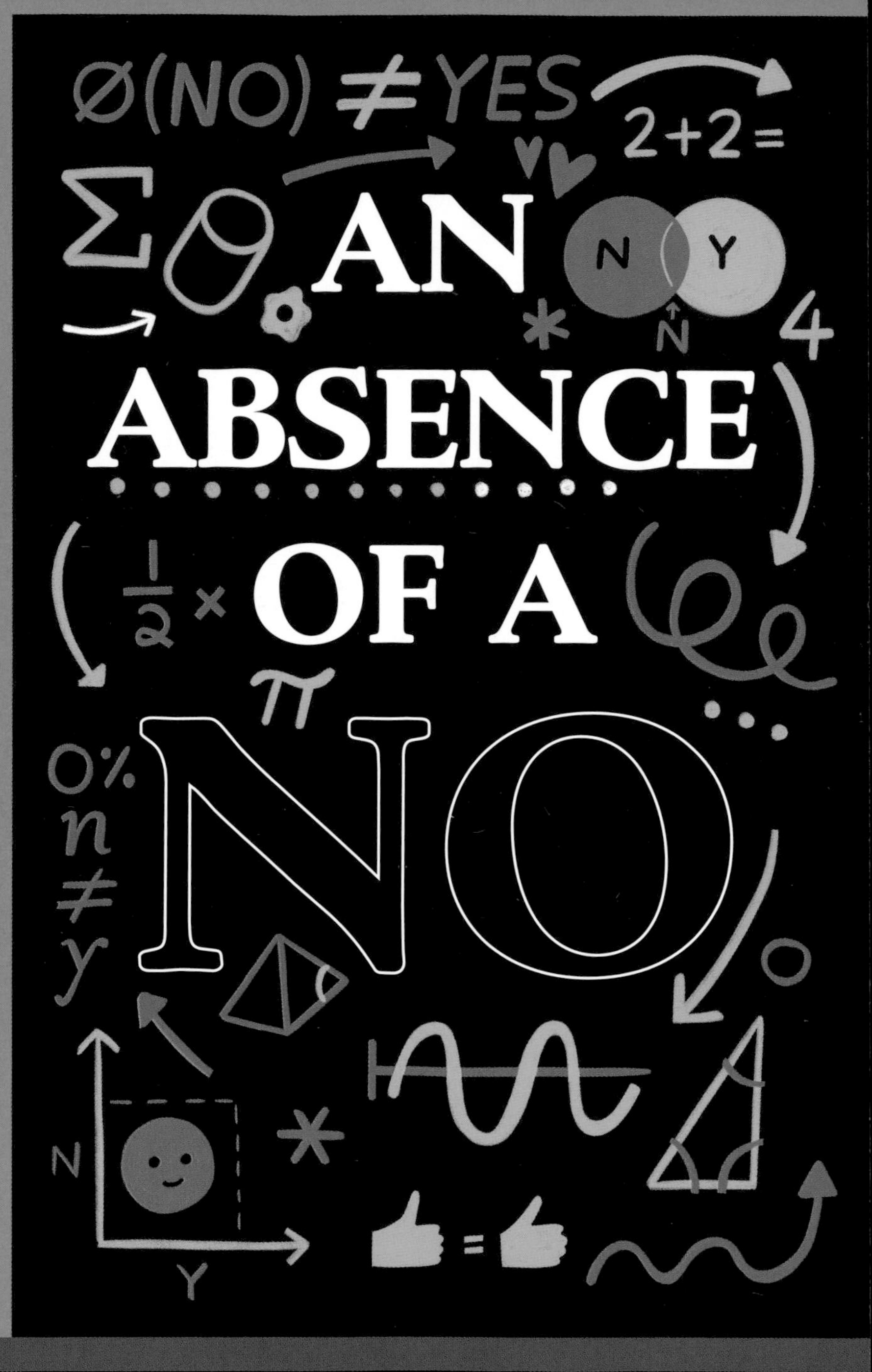

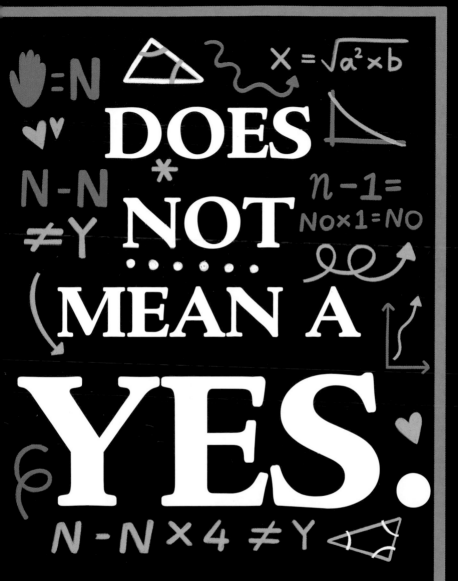

# DOES NOT MEAN A YES.

If everyone buys this book (I hope they do, because my pizza habit isn't cheap) and learns how to ask consensually, then maybe we won't have to say no. But until they do, we will sometimes need to say "no" to people. Here's how...

*How to Say NO #1*

# YOU SHOULD ONLY HAVE TO SAY NO ONCE

Increase your chances of your "no" being heard by saying it clearly. You could perhaps put your hand out in front of you at the same time and say "no." If they keep asking, then keep saying "no" each time they ask. Think about getting help if they aren't listening to you or moving into a more public space where people can see you. If they are doing it via their phone, you could say "no" and mute or block them. If they are being persistent to the point of harassing you, you could perhaps get a trusted adult to help you. They could either intervene on your behalf or help you to report it.

## How to Say NO #2
# FIELD WHAT THEY SAY AND THROW IT BACK

Another thing you can do is repeat back what they're saying and say "no." An example of this is, "I know you want to go out with me, but I don't want to. So, no." You're fielding, or catching, what they're saying, and throwing it back to them. It shows that you've heard them, but you're telling them what you want. If it's safe, you could add a bit of humor if you feel like it.

*How to Say NO #3*

## HUMOR MIGHT WORK

Sometimes, saying something funny can defuse a difficult situation and gives everyone the option of backing out. Especially if you've already said "no" and they haven't heard it. If you search the internet for "funny ways to say no," there are lots of different responses (and it shows what a problem it is for lots of people). I would go with, "it's a no from me," and be all Simon Cowell about it. Or, "I've consulted with my legal team and they say no—sorry about that."

## How to Say NO #4
# TURN THE TABLES

If they try to make you feel guilty about saying "no," you might want to turn the tables on them. So if they say, "if you were my friend...," or "if you loved me you'd...," then you can turn that around and say it right back at them. If they were your friend or if they loved you, then they would treat you more consensually. This isn't a book about relationships, but remember that love isn't just something you say, it's something you do. Doing things consensually is a way of being loving to people. Making someone do something they don't want to do, isn't.

*How to Say NO #5*
## HAVE A SAYING READY

Try having a saying ready, too.
I have a t-shirt that has "SORRY
(NOT SORRY)" in big letters because
I like that expression. You could say,
"It's a no—sorry (not sorry) about
that." Pick a phrase that you keep
repeating over and over again,
so it becomes as easy as saying
"Ummmm" or "I dunno."

## GETTING ASSERTIVE

Lastly, sometimes you might have to get really assertive with someone if they are being very unreasonable with you. Below is a four-point action plan on how to do this:

1. Point out their terrible behavior (like them not listening to your "no").

2. Say how it's making you feel (maybe scared, angry, sad, or disappointed).

3. Tell them what you want them to do (listen or stop).

4. Tell them what will happen if they don't (you might unfriend them or report them to someone).

All of this can be really difficult and examples of when our agency can be affected by someone else. But although we are being put in the unpleasant position of having to say it, saying "no" can sometimes be really good for us. Remember that we are saying "no" to them, and "yes" to us. That in itself gives us agency.

Remember that even after all this, if we don't manage to say "no," it doesn't make it okay for someone to treat us non-consensually. We shouldn't be put in the position of having to say "no." They are the person in the wrong, not us.

# Chapter Six

# Consensual greetings

In life, there are some things we do that we don't ask for in the same way that we might order a pizza. Greetings is one of them.

Handshakes, fist bumps, nods, salutes, hugs, kisses. The different kinds of physical interactions we do with different people when we meet them. They happen all the time, but have you ever thought about how to do them consensually? Don't worry—just like with pizza, I've spent way too much time thinking about it. You're welcome!

Spoiler alert: it's also going to be a metaphor for sex. But for the moment, don't think about sex. I'll tell you when we get to the sex bit. For now, if you could keep thinking about greetings that would be great.

# THE GREETINGS WE "SHOULD" DO

Imagine that you are meeting someone for the first time. How do you greet them? To save awkwardness, there are usually social customs for how we are meant to do that. For example, in the UK, where I live, we are supposed to shake hands. In different parts of the world it might be different. It might be kisses, fist bumps, hugs, a non-contact greeting like a wave, a salute, or a hands together acknowledgment. But crucially, there is usually some local custom for what kind of greeting we should do.

There are usually quite strict rules on how to do the greeting, too. In the UK, the unspoken rules with handshakes say that we should be right-handed, have a medium to firm grip, a dry hand, go up and down for two or three seconds, and then you're done. There could even be a bit of eye contact, but not too much. Again, there are rules about how you're supposed to do different greetings in different countries, and even in different parts of a country. What are yours?

This way of doing handshakes works for lots of people, but it doesn't work for everyone. For example, left-handed people will very rarely get to shake hands with their left hand. Some people find that handshakes can be a bit too firm or a bit too soft for them, because there's no agreement

about what "medium-firm" feels like. So some people will feel like their hands are being crushed, but others will feel like their hand has come into contact with a wet halibut.

Also it's not clear whether we are meant to change our handshake depending on whose hand we are shaking. How do we do it if we are shaking the hand of someone with a different gender to us, or if someone's hand is a lot bigger or smaller than ours? What about shaking hands with someone who is older or younger than us?

Some people describe themselves as "huggers." They might decide that a handshake isn't really enough of a greeting, and might put their arms out to upgrade it to a hug.

## That's great if the other person wanted the same, but what if they didn't?

News flash: some people really, really hate hugs (and that's okay).

Remember when I talked about Should Stories? As you can see, this applies to greetings, too. There's a Should Story for what kinds of greetings we should be doing and how we should be doing them, even though we can't agree on exactly how. Should Stories about greetings make us think that we have to greet everyone the same way. **It can lead to us taking part in greetings that we feel like we should do, rather than we want to do.**

Some of the things that happen in the greeting might not be consensual: like going in for a hug, using a grip that's too firm or using a finger to stroke the other person's hand in a handshake (which sounds gross, so don't do that).

Why can't we do a handshake that is more consensual? Is it possible to express what we want from a greeting? Can we even work out what kind of greeting we want? Are we able to not only talk about how to greet each other, but also be able to do the greeting in a way that is mutually more fun and nice?

## NEGOTIATING A GREETING

So, how can we do that? We could start by asking and giving each other options. We could say "Handshake? Hug? Or kiss?" when we first meet someone. Even better would be to say something like, "How would you feel about having a greeting of some kind? I'd be up for a handshake, a fist bump, or a hug, but do you have any other greetings you particularly like?"

If you both agree to stick with the handshake, then maybe you could negotiate which hand you might want to use (if both hands are available for you both to use). Would you prefer a completely dry hand or is a slightly clammy hand okay? How firm do you want it to be? You could negotiate it from a 10, which is bone-crushing, to a 1, which is the wet halibut. Do you want to go up and down or side to side? How big do you want the movement to be? How long will the greeting last for? **But you could also just, you know, not.**

It'd be great if we could do all of this, but it's not something that I'd do with people I don't know. However, I have negotiated greetings with people I'm close to. This has ranged from a firm handshake, a kiss on the cheek (each other's right cheek), a kiss on the lips (steady now), and a hug with a firm squeeze of about two or three seconds.

I use this activity when I teach people about consent. I ask people to try to negotiate greetings with each other and a lot of people have told me what they thought about it. Some thought it was a bit strange at first, but then they really got into it.

Others liked the fact that they could spend a bit of time finding out more from each other about what they both wanted.

Some handshakes developed into something more elaborate and silly. Others negotiated hugs or another kind of greeting.

Some of them enjoyed being able to choose their greetings together. They liked that they could meet each other's needs and have their needs met. They also thought it was more fun. But others thought it was too awkward—it raised their expectations of the handshake, there was too much pressure, and it all went wrong.

Maybe this is something you could try with a friend or family member. Try negotiating next time you have a greeting with someone and see how it goes.

# HOW TO DO A MORE CONSENSUAL GREETING

So there's the Should Story about how to do a greeting. It's sometimes okay, but it doesn't always give us what we want from a greeting, and can sometimes be non-consensual. The other option (think Infinity Pizza™) is to talk about our wants and needs from a greeting, negotiate what kind of greeting might meet those needs for us both, and then do a more consensual and mutual greeting. A lot of people would like that, but it's also too awkward for a lot of people to actually put into practice.

## Is there a way to get the best of both worlds and have a greeting that is more mutual and consensual?

No, there is absolutely no way that a greeting can be consensual. Only joking! Of course there is.

Say a group of you are going out (for pizza) and you are meeting a friend of a friend for the first time. How are you going to greet them when you've never met them before? The thing to do is to slow everything down and concentrate on what is actually happening.

Are they moving toward you or away from you?

Are they standing back like they just want to nod their heads and not have a physical greeting, or are they moving toward you for some kind of physical greeting?

If their hand is coming out, is it stretched out like they want a handshake or is their hand bunched up like they want a fist bump? Do they look like they want to go for a hug?

If you move toward them first, are they moving toward you or have they taken a step back in response?

How do you feel about that? If you're not feeling it, you could put your arms down. If you're looking to do a hug, where are their arms in response to your movement?

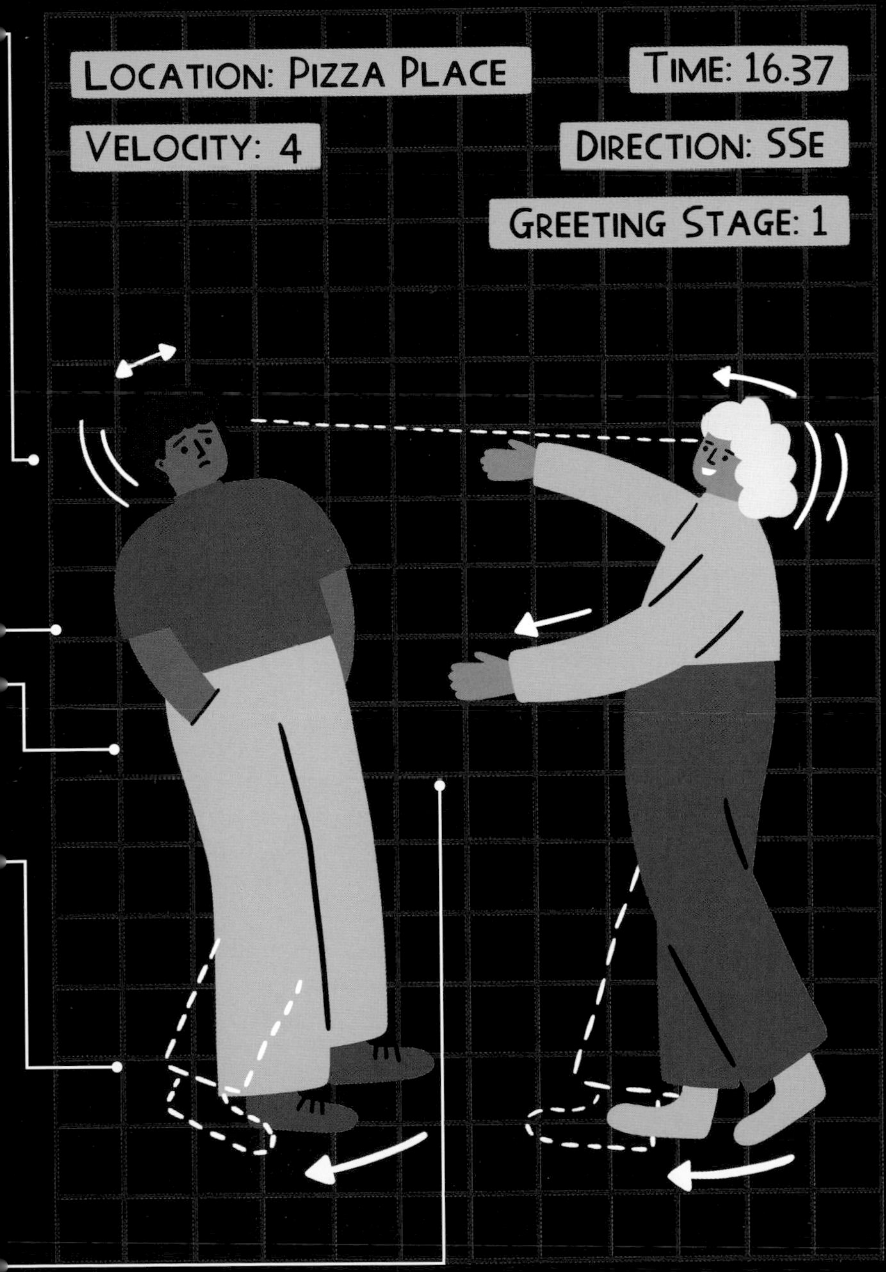

LOCATION: PIZZA PLACE    TIME: 16.37

VELOCITY: 4    DIRECTION: SSE

GREETING STAGE: 1

# Remember: it's always better to not do something

If it looks like you are going to have a greeting, **PAY ATTENTION** to the moment of contact. So if it's a handshake, try to adjust the firmness to match what they are doing. That way, it's not going to be too firm or too soft. Try to **NOTICE** if there is resistance in their hand—this might tell you that you're going in the wrong direction for them. Also notice when the handshake starts and when it stops. When does the other person want to loosen their hand? Can you manage to do that at the same time?

Notice whether each of you say anything during it and whether they are flinching or finding the greeting uncomfortable.

than to do it if you're not sure
how the other person is feeling.

**CHECK IN** with their facial expressions afterward to see whether this was something that was okay for them. Hopefully if they've read this book, they'll be doing this for you, too. Perhaps it might have been a really good greeting because you were trying to make it as okay as you could for both of you.

Next time you greet someone, try it! Slow everything down and see if you can aim for a mutually consensual greeting. It's hard to do because greetings only last for a couple of seconds, but it's a way of bringing more consent into our daily lives. It's also a way of practicing for other interactions. Yes, that's right. We're going to talk about sex.

Chapter Seven

# The sex bit

All that stuff about greetings is important
because I think we need to be doing better
at consent all the time in all parts of life.
But it's also super relevant to sex, too.

Like with greetings, sex is often not something that people ask questions about in the same way that we ask someone what game they want to play, what show to watch or, you know, pizza. The following section will look at ideas about how you can bring in more choice and freedom when it comes to sex. We'll also talk about what it is about sex that makes this so tricky.

This next bit will feature most of the sexual content in the book, so it's okay if you aren't ready to learn about sex yet. **Either skip ahead, or put the book down for a bit. Either way is totally fine.**

# SHOULD STORIES ABOUT SEX

Remember how I was saying that there are stories about greetings that say we "should" do them, and that we "should" do them in a particular way? In other words, Should Stories.

WELL, IT'S THE SAME FOR SEX.

*One story says that everyone is interested in having sex at some point.*

*There's another story that says that sex is a particular set of acts in a particular order.*

*And there's a story that we don't need to talk about it if we meet the right person.*

**A**ll these stories are NOT TRUE.

Not everyone is interested in having sex. I won't go into much detail about sexualities here, but some people don't experience sexual attraction, feelings, or desires. They're just not into it. This is called asexuality. There are variations of this where people are more interested in sex if they are interested in a person. But ultimately, not everyone is interested in having sex.

Some people are not interested in having sex yet. Many people want to wait until they are older before they have sex, or wait until they are in a relationship, or even when they get married. These are all completely fine ways to feel about sex. It's also fine if people are really super interested in having sex and being sexually attracted to people.

However, the Should Story would have us believe that you have to be interested in sex, not too much, but just enough.

**AND I HATE THAT SHOULD STORY.**

## SHOULD STORY ABOUT WHAT SEX IS

The Should Story about what sex is also puts pressure on us. If I was to say that there was a picture of two people having sex on the next page (there isn't), what do you imagine you might see? I think that most people would imagine that it would be a man and a woman, usually with the man on top. They'd be naked, in a bed, the man would have a penis and it would be inside the woman's vagina. **Any other kind of sex, like kissing, stroking, or licking is considered "foreplay" and isn't part of "real sex."**

This is what we are told sex is. It's what "counts" as sex. We see it in sex advice books, Hollywood sex scenes, TV sex scenes, and porn sex scenes (as well as a lot of other kinds of sex, too). It's what we're often taught in sex ed class (which is usually just "don't get someone pregnant" and, ummmm, that's it).

This story is wrong and really quite a problematic way of thinking. It leaves out people who can't have that kind of sex or who don't want to have that kind of sex. People who are disabled or those who identify as LGBTQIA+ (lesbian, gay, bi, trans, queer, intersex, asexual, and many others) are often excluded from this very narrow idea of what sex is.

A lot of people don't or can't enjoy this kind of sex. This sex Should Story puts a lot of pressure on us to have sex in a way that we might not be able to have or might not enjoy.

When we say that sex is this one thing, it means that we are either "doing it" or "not doing it," which, as we have seen, is not much choice at all. Often when people have sex, they are so into the idea of "doing it" that they are just following the story of what sex is, rather than paying attention to the needs of the person they are doing it with. Not exactly Infinity Pizza™, is it?

# SHOULD STÖRY *

1.

2.

3.

4.

*Of course if you are going to have this kind of sex, it's good to use a condom.

# What if sex was many things?

As with greetings, the story we have been taught about what sex is and how we should do it can make it harder to enjoy it consensually. So instead of sex just being one thing, that we either do or don't do, what if it was many, many different things? What if it was like Infinity Pizza™, where you could choose your own bases, your own sauces, and your own toppings? What if you could have whatever kind of pizza you wanted, and you and the person you were having sex with could figure that out together?

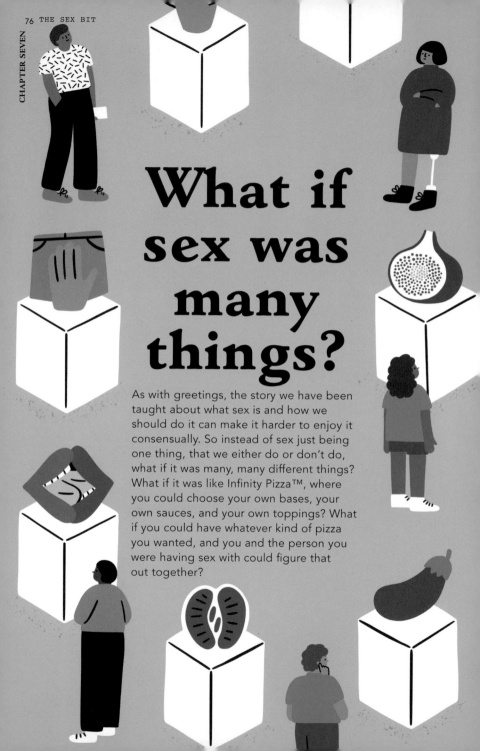

Well, good news: it is.

Imagine a graph. On the left-hand side, there's all the parts of someone's body that could be touched. At the bottom, there's all the parts of someone's body that could touch another person in every way possible. For example: using your fingers to stroke someone's hair, face, or knee. Or using your tongue to lick their nipple, lips, or armpit. There would be sooooo many different options, and that's just from touch. As well as touching, sex is about the things that we might say, hear, see, or imagine.

Of course, just like choosing a pizza, the choice can be overwhelming. That's fine. You don't have to like everything and it's more than likely that you won't. There also might be some things that you don't know if you like or not. The key is to try and find out what is going to work for you and someone else, consensually. This does mean that you need to do some talking before anything happens. As we found with greetings, talking about what we want from a situation and then negotiating how to do it can be very tricky. But it's even more important to be able to do some of this with sex than it is with greetings.

# The crucial thing to remember here is that sex isn't just one thing.

# It's also not one thing that someone does to another person. It's lots of different things that we can do by ourselves, but also with other people. It's an activity to take part in together.

I need to point out that underage sex is against the law. Search for "legal age to have sex" to find out the law in your state. Across the world, it's usually between 16 and 18 for all genders (sadly, in a small number of countries, it's illegal to have sex with someone of the same gender at all). In the US, it's unlikely that you will get in trouble if you're just under the legal age, are both around the same age, and your relationship is consensual and not abusive. This applies to any sexual activity with another person. The law exists to protect young people from abuse, particularly the younger person. Okay, I've stopped wagging my finger now.

Here are some tips about how you can get started.

## TALKING ABOUT TALKING

There are lots of different kinds of sex and you get to choose which, if any, you would like to do. But how might you talk about what kinds of sex you want? And how do you negotiate it with someone? A lot of people feel really anxious talking about sex. It's partly because they might not have had very much practice at choosing what they want to do. But it's also because sex can be difficult to talk about for a lot of people.

Sadly, there is a lot of stigma and shame when it comes to talking about sex. Some people get more stigma for talking about it than others (more about this later). For many of us, we were taught that sex is something we shouldn't really mention because talking about it is rude. But when young people are thinking of actually having sex, adults sometimes say, "You need to be able to talk about it," or "If you can't talk about it, you shouldn't be doing it." Which is all very confusing and conflicting.

Your ability to talk about what you want or don't want from sex is going to be related to what kind of sex education you've had. If you had really good sex education, either at home or at school, you'll have had more practice using the words and will feel less awkward about it. If, however, you haven't had such great sex education, then you might notice that you are embarrassed to talk about it. If the whole idea just fills your head with cringey thoughts, it might be good to say that to the person you're interested in having sex with.

Try, "Hi, I'm very interested in having some sexy times but I have no idea how to talk about how, what, or when. Can we chat about that?"

Talking about the fact that it's awkward can make some of the awkwardness go away. It's better for you both to acknowledge that it's awkward and that you don't quite know what to do next, than to say nothing at all. I think that it would be better for people who have had lots of sex to be more like this, too. It means that you can start to have a conversation about how you begin.

If we're trying to be as consensual as possible at all times, that includes how we talk about having sex. Some people can talk about what they want quite clearly, others less so. You could:

• Agree that one person starts with some suggestions of things that they might like to do.

• Start slow and do a couple of things. See how it goes and chat about it afterward.

• Just see how things go and agree to communicate with each other during it.

• Talk about everything you'd like to try and how you'd like to do it. You could do this either by text or in person.

• Chat about how much talking during sex is okay. For example, you might decide that checking in with each other is good from time to time, but not all the time.

• Agree how you'll say no. For example, "I'll just stop if I'm not into it anymore."

• Try the Should Story for sex (if that works for you), but be slow and let each other stop or change things.

# TALKING ABOUT EXACTLY WHAT YOU WANT TO DO

Like we discussed earlier, pizza places can give us lots of choices by offering different kinds of pizza. To make our choices easier, we can do that with sex, too. So instead of trying to choose from the infinite number of sex things that can be experienced, it might be better to choose from a menu of things that people often enjoy when they have sex.

Opposite is a list of things that people might like. For each one, you can go through and ask yourself and each other if they are a "no", "maybe," or "yes". Or you could give them a score on a scale of -10 --------- 0 ---------- +10.

Remember that not everyone likes all of these things—that's the point. They are not in any particular order (I don't want to tell a Should Story).

- Knee stroking
- Ear nibbling or licking
- Deep kissing with tongues
- Massaging each other naked
- Gentle kissing on the cheek
- Kissing on the lips
- Stroking wrists and hands
- Using a mouth on a penis or clitoris
- Stroking naked nipples
- Kissing face, eyes, neck, ears, and cheeks
- Solo masturbation next to each other
- Having vaginal sex (with fingers, penis, or sex toys)
- Stroking a penis or clitoris directly

- Having anal sex (with fingers, penis, or sex toys)
- Touching chest, bum or other parts of the body with clothes on
- Gently biting
- Sending a text saying they are turned on
- Holding hands
- Wearing an eye mask
- Giving a shoulder rub with clothes on
- Tickling
- Stroking the penis or vulva through underpants
- Rubbing genitals together
- Spooning (lying up close against their back)
- Sending a sexy pic (it's only legal to do this if you are over 18*)
- Dry humping (rubbing up against each other with clothes on)
- Sharing sexy fantasies

*The police are not likely to investigate if the pics were sent consensually. The law is there to protect under 18s from having their pics shared without their consent.

Talking about sex makes things a bit easier because you can at least have some ideas of how to begin. Just like with pizza, you can choose an option and then have something taken off that you don't want. For example, just like you could take mushrooms off a veggie pizza, you could choose to kiss but without tongues. When you get more experienced and learn more about sex, then you could broaden out the list of things you might be into and create your own much bigger menu. Or you could create a very small list of things on your menu, and that would be okay too.

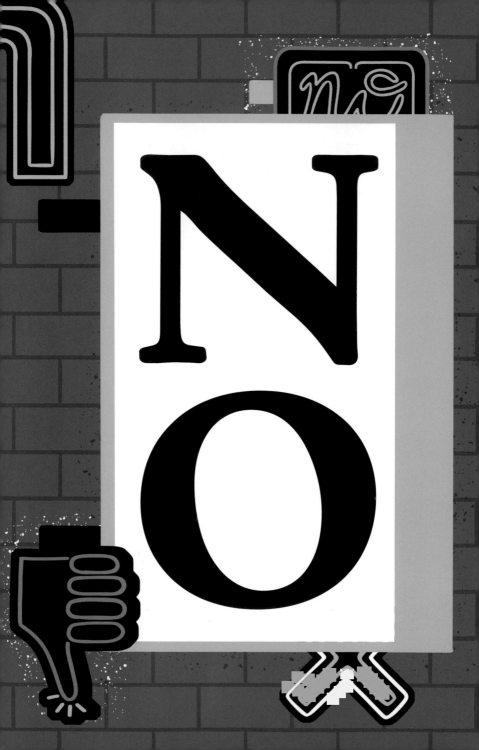

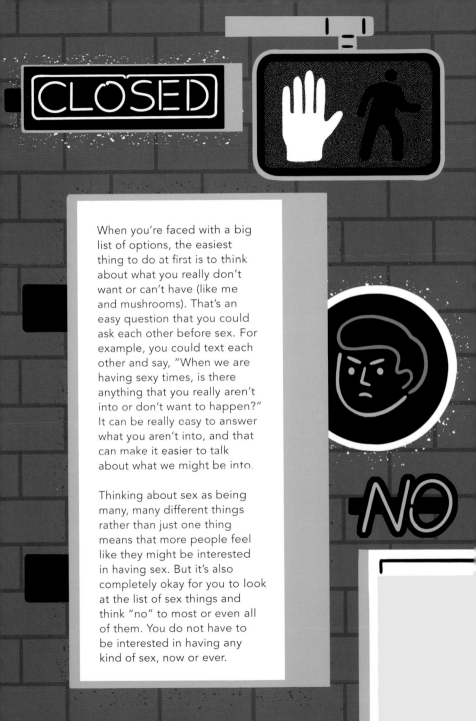

When you're faced with a big list of options, the easiest thing to do at first is to think about what you really don't want or can't have (like me and mushrooms). That's an easy question that you could ask each other before sex. For example, you could text each other and say, "When we are having sexy times, is there anything that you really aren't into or don't want to happen?" It can be really easy to answer what you aren't into, and that can make it easier to talk about what we might be into.

Thinking about sex as being many, many different things rather than just one thing means that more people feel like they might be interested in having sex. But it's also completely okay for you to look at the list of sex things and think "no" to most or even all of them. You do not have to be interested in having any kind of sex, now or ever.

We often don't know if we are going to be into something before we do it. One of the ways that we learn about our likes and dislikes is by having a try. However, we can also make a pretty good guess about what we might feel ready for or what we're interested in based on how we feel about our body, and whether we have had sex much by ourselves. This is called "solo sex"—touching your body in ways that feel sexy, like masturbation.

So when you're thinking about the different kinds of sex that you might be into, it's okay to be unsure. You might want to learn more about something first, or you might need certain things to happen to make you more comfortable. For example, them washing their hands before, keeping some clothes on, or using a condom for oral sex.

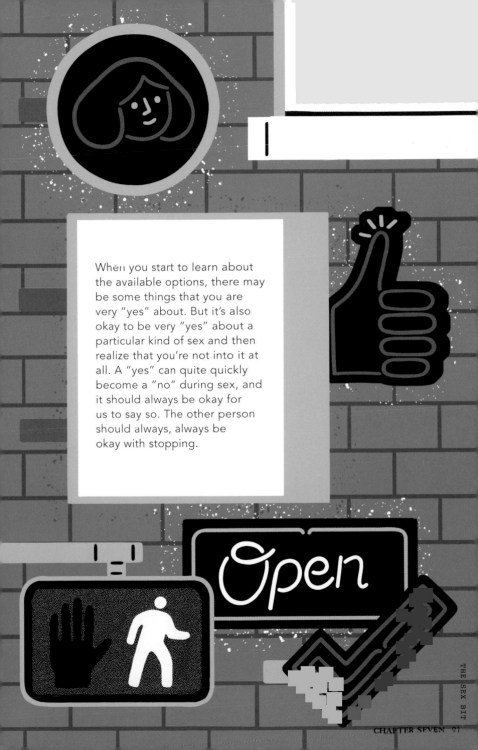

When you start to learn about the available options, there may be some things that you are very "yes" about. But it's also okay to be very "yes" about a particular kind of sex and then realize that you're not into it at all. A "yes" can quite quickly become a "no" during sex, and it should always be okay for us to say so. The other person should always, always be okay with stopping.

Open

## SCORING SYSTEM

Thinking about different kinds of sex and whether you say "yes," "no," or "maybe" gives us quite a lot of choice, but we can increase our choices even more. You could chat about how interested you are in different things by rating each kind of sexual activity. For example:

**-10----------0----------+10**

-10: I really don't want to.
0: I'm not sure, meh, don't mind either way.
+10: I'm really keen on doing this.

Being clear about how much we want to do something means that we can think about who we are doing something for—whether it's for yourself, for the other person, or for each other equally.

If you were +2 on say, knee stroking (hey, that's a thing), and the other person was +9, then you might be quite happy for them to get their knee out because you knew they would really like it. It's okay to enjoy doing something for someone else, and if they enjoy it, then our enjoyment might also increase. It also means that you can ask the other person for something you might like, such as having your neck stroked like a cat.

For consent to happen, we shouldn't have to do something that we don't want to do. So if we were a -2 on the knee stroking, the other person should take that as a "no" unless we say otherwise. But so long as we are somewhere on a + scale, it's okay for us to have different levels of enthusiasm for

different kinds of sex. Otherwise, we might miss out on the sex we want to have.

If a time comes when you're ready to talk about this, you can have these kinds of conversations in person before you have sex, or in texts before you have sex.

## TEXTING

Sending texts is a great way of communicating what you like or don't like, and you can spend time getting the wording right.

It's also a good way of asking for something specific or for pointing out what you really aren't into. If you do this in combination with talking about what sex you want then this can be really effective.

You can even tell each other sexy stories—which also counts as sex, even if you aren't together.

It's also a great way to communicate after sex. It can be a lovely to talk about the sex, what went well, and what you'd like to do differently next time. Think of it like a post-game analysis.

So you can send texts as a method of communication, but if you are sending a sexy text (sext) remember that this is also a sexual activity. If you are sending texts that are sexual (rather than just communicating), then make sure this is being done consensually and safely. So all of this chapter is relevant for sexts, too.

# HOW TO COMMUNICATE

Whether you are choosing to follow the Should Story a bit, just starting out with a couple of things, or have fully worked out how you're going to have sex, it's crucially important that you're able to communicate during sex too. **Because consent needs to happen all the time and all throughout sex, not just at the beginning.**

Even if you can't or don't want to talk about everything before sex, it's important to be able to communicate during sex. Even if you've talked about what you would like to do beforehand, it's okay for people to change their mind at any time. So here are some tips on how to communicate. It's a bit like when we were talking about how to make greetings more consensual by looking at body language— I call this "micro-communication."

These tips don't work for everyone and not everyone will be able to do them all (for example, if you have difficulties seeing or hearing), so there are lots of different ways to communicate you can try. And remember that different kinds of responses mean different things

with different people. You might need to use different methods of communication during sex to understand what is going on for the other person.

Good communication also means that you might need to slow things down and check in with each other regularly. Sometimes that might not be the "sexy" thing to do, but it's definitely the right thing to do. Sometimes in order to have consensual sex, you need to not have sex.

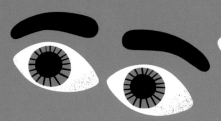

We can sometimes tell from looking into someone's eyes whether they are into something—especially if it's accompanied by a nod of the head, a smile, or an "Oh yeah." Sometimes people might make direct eye contact as if to say "yes" and sometimes as if to say "No, I'm serious, this has to stop."

It doesn't always mean the same thing for the same person.

Because people's sex faces are different and can be confusing, it's important to check in with them. Being able to see people's facial expressions or able to hear

# EYE CONTACT

If someone is looking away, it might mean that they aren't that into what is happening. But it could also mean that they are in their own space and having a great time. It could also mean that they really don't like eye contact. Some people find that eye contact is a bit too intense for them.

what they are saying (or lip-read what they are saying) is important if you are new to having sex with each other. This is why I recommend having sex in a face-to-face position in the beginning.

Eye contact means different things so it's useful to pay attention to their body language. If you have any doubts, stop and ask how they are feeling.

If you can't see their facial expression very well, either because it's dark or because you can't see, you could try some of these other methods...

# NOISES

Sometimes people make lots of noise when they're enjoying sex, but sometimes they don't. Some people might be more shy about being vocal than others. This means that if someone is quiet during sex, then things might still be going well for them.

The level of noise varies for everyone: it's a very personal thing. Sometimes a pleasure sound can sound like a pain sound, and that can be very confusing when you are new to sex.

So if you're confused about what someone's noise means, it's a good idea to stop and check in with them. It's always better to be cautious.

Just because someone isn't shouting "no" or "stop" doesn't mean that they are happy continuing.

# WORDS

If you are doing the start slow and "see how it goes" approach to sex, you could actually talk during it. Once things get going, you can use short phrases to say what you want.

## You can also encourage your partner to do what feels good.

Short phrases are easier to say. You can also whisper in someone's ear, which may also be easier. Phrases like, "Can you move?", or "Just there," or "Bit softer/harder/faster/slower," or "Keep going," or "Slow down," or "Shhhh," or "Whelp," or "Bingo." That kind of thing.

Also remember to listen to their breathing. A sharp intake of breath might mean that something hurts, or was a surprise. A long exhale might mean that someone is really relaxed and enjoying it. However, if someone falls asleep because they are so relaxed (or if they are sleepy from alcohol, for example) you must stop.

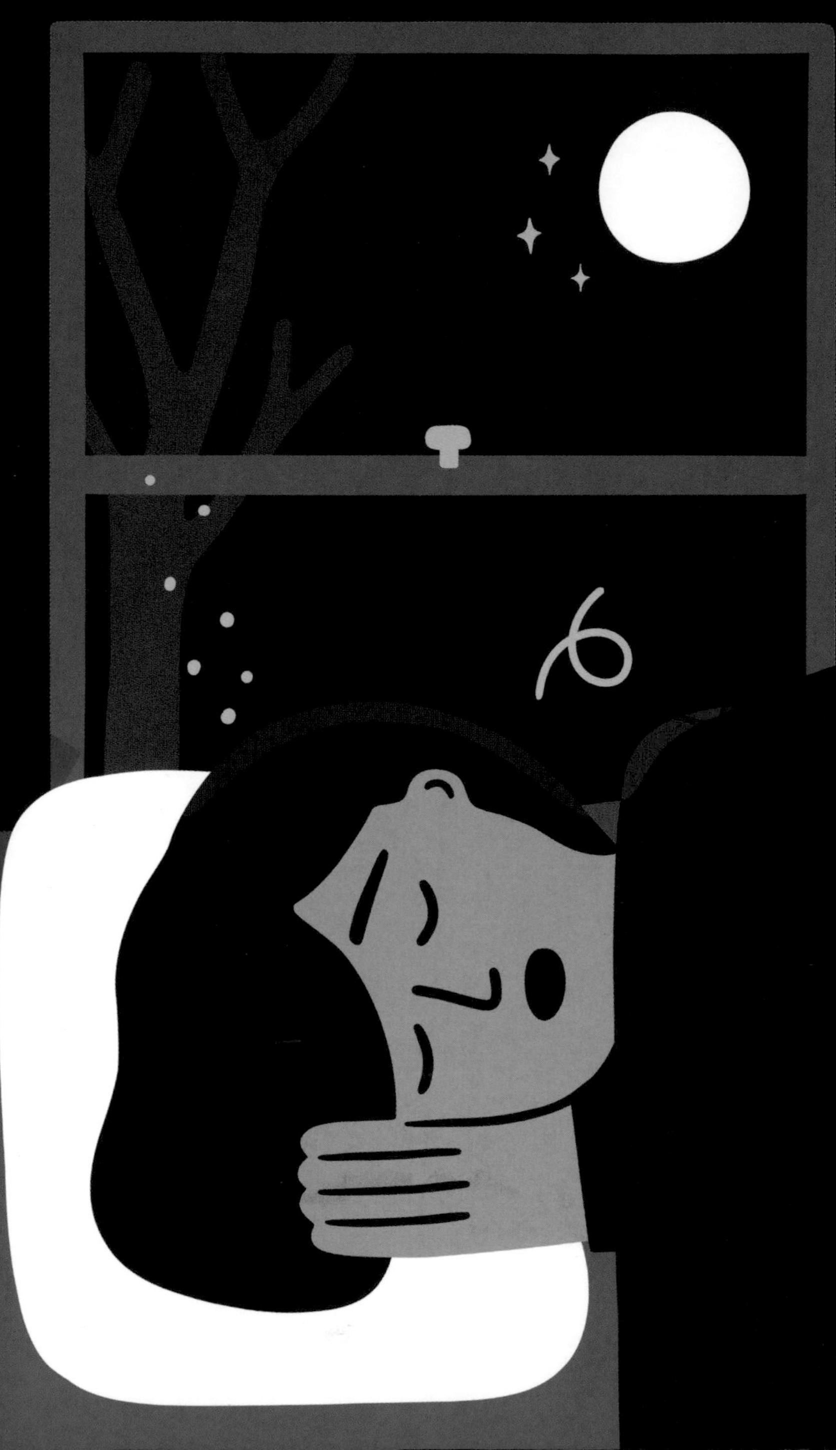

**Because someone can't consent if they aren't awake.**

# HANDS

You're allowed to use your hands if you want—sex isn't soccer. You can move someone's hand if they're touching you in a place or in a way you aren't keen on. Or you can put their hand on your hand and guide them to where you like to be touched and how.

A "tap" on the shoulder might mean that they've had enough of that thing. Or a hand being placed on your chest to hold you back might mean "Give me a sec." If someone is holding you in place that might mean "right there" or "just like that" or "don't stop."

## Talking first about what these different hand signals mean to you would be a great idea.

Especially if you don't like talking during sex, or if you have disabilities that make communicating by sight or sound difficult.

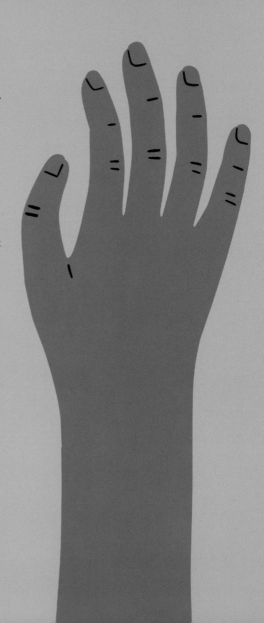

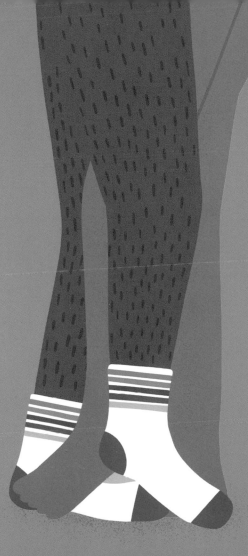

If people's bodies move toward each other or copy each other, this is a sign that they are enjoying what the other is doing. Remember that even if someone looks like they are physically aroused, that doesn't always mean they want to have, or want to continue having, sex. If someone moves away, becomes very passive, or leaves the room, it's a sign that they aren't happy.

Look out for if people suddenly twitch or tense up. This might be a sign that something is wrong. If someone starts to gradually tremble or shake then that might be a sign that they are enjoying it.

However, everyone reacts in different ways and that's true when sex is consensual and also not consensual (sexual assault).

# BODIES

# WHEN
# TO
# STOP

**Here are times when you need to kill the mood, stop everything, and actually talk.**

• If they look unhappy or aren't engaging.

• If something has changed during sex. For example, if the condom has broken or come off.

• If you want to do something different to what you've already done.

• If sex is getting uncomfortable or painful for you or you think it might be for them.

Remember, someone should only have to say "no" or "stop" or "wait" once. If someone says this to you, you must stop.

## Chapter Eight

# Meh, let's not

**It should always be okay to just not do something, but often it isn't okay.**

As well as there being some things that most of us have to do (like school or work), there's often a lot of pressure on us to do what someone else is asking us to do. That can come from people we are close to who want us to do something (and it may be that we want to please them more than we want to please ourselves), but it can also come from society.

For one thing, when everyone else is doing something, or when we think everyone else is doing something, then there can be a lot of peer pressure. "Everyone else seems to be doing this, so maybe I should do it too"—you know, that kind of thing. For me, this happens if I'm trying to cross a road and a load of people next to me start to cross. When they all move, I start to move too, without thinking about whether it's actually safe to cross or not. The fact that peer pressure can happen to me, a 44-year-old who writes about consent, means that it can happen to anyone.

Another source of pressure is the whole, "Well, once you've done this step, you should take the next step." It can be sex, relationships

> It should be fine to just stay on the step that you're comfortable.

generally, or even greetings again. For example, for a lot of people the Should Story is that you do handshakes when you don't know a person so well, and then when you've met them a few times, you take the next step and do hugs. I'm usually pretty chill with that to be honest, but a friend of mine really hates hugs and there's always a lot of pressure on him to do it because it's "the next step." It should be fine to just stay on the step where you're comfortable.

Pressure also comes from stories—in movies, TV, songs, or the internet. Like a spooky story when there's a group of people and they should go into an old, haunted-looking house. Or in a romantic comedy when one of the characters should

propose marriage to someone. Or where someone should confront the school bully by themselves. Because we are supposed to feel brave and courageous, go inside that haunted house, get down on one knee, or learn karate to defend ourselves from the bully. But often in life, it's better to just... not. Not doing something can actually be the brave thing to do.

Pressure can often mean that it feels easier to do something rather than not—like taking part in a hug just because someone is putting their arms out, or watching a movie we don't like because everyone else does. But doing something because of pressure can hurt us and other people because we aren't thinking about what we (or they) want or need.

## Practicing consent is better than doing the thing.

And that's not consensual. It's the Should Story again—something that we "should" do rather than what we might or might not want to do. It's really, really powerful and I'm not joking when I say that it's something that I still struggle with (again, I am 44).

So actually, the brave thing to do is to have conversations, give each other options, check in with each other, and give each other and ourselves a way out of doing something. Practicing consent is better than doing the thing. If we were really doing consent with ourselves and others, we would be doing things a lot less (or doing lots of different kinds of things). All the ideas I've given you should help with that.

Have conversations, give each other options, check in with each other, and give each other and ourselves a way out of doing something.

# DRINK AND DRUGS

A lot of people feel that they need to drink or take drugs before they have sex (remember that underage drinking is illegal and most drugs are illegal altogether). This might be to relax them, give them confidence, or help them feel less cringe about the whole thing. But if everyone had proper sex education and was taught about consent, then they might not feel like they have to.

Although people might think that drink and drugs can make it easier for them to have sex, it actually makes it harder to have consent. As we've been talking about throughout the book, consent is about freedom, choices, and agency. The more we might drink or take, the less agency we might end up having, particularly if we don't know what we are doing, are dazed and out of it, or getting sleepy.

If we are drunk or high, it's also a lot harder to communicate properly in the way that we need to, to make sex consensual. It can be hard for us to communicate, but it can also be harder for us to accurately understand what the other person is saying to us. Remember that being drunk or high is no excuse for something non-consensual happening—in fact, it's often proof that consent can't have been given.

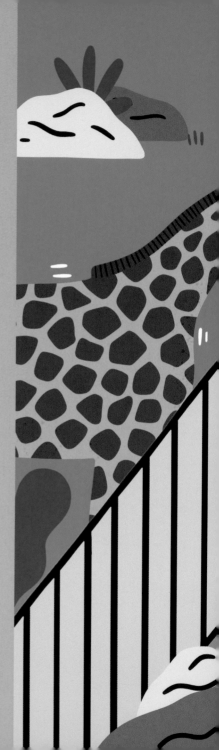

## WHAT IF SOMETHING NON-CONSENSUAL HAPPENS?

Non-consensual things happen all the time, either to us or caused by us to others. Sometimes it doesn't cause any real harm and it wasn't intentional—like me bumping into someone in the street. I say sorry, they hold their hand up to say, "it's fine," and we carry on. However, sometimes people can be harmed from non-consensual actions in a much more serious way. What can we do if we have been affected by these actions? Read on for some options.

# WE CAN REPORT IT

To make someone responsible for what they did, as well as getting support, you can report what happened. If it was a crime, such as assault, sexual assault, or rape, you can report it to the police. You can also report it if you go to a medical center to get treatment by telling the medical professional you wish to report the crime. There are some contacts at the back of this book that you may find helpful if you ever find yourself in a non-consensual situation.

If the incident happened at school, college, or work, you could also try telling someone there. There will usually be someone in these institutions that you can report to. They should have a clear policy about what it is they will do, what support you can expect, and what might happen to the perpetrator (whoever did the thing).

# SUPPORT

It's probably a good idea to get some support from someone who you trust and who is wise (and who is not the perpetrator) to help you. It can be really difficult to cope with our reactions to non-consensual stuff, and our feelings, thoughts, and actions can be confusing. Sometimes we fight or run away in order to keep ourselves safe. When we are under attack, our bodies take over and we don't really get any control over how we respond. So having someone there for you is super important.

If you are being called on to help someone who's been through something non-consensual, then the most important thing is to be as consensual toward them as possible. At the beginning of this book, we looked at agency and freedom as an antidote to things that have happened to us we didn't want. So if you are supporting someone, try to find out what kinds of support they might want, either by asking, giving options, or being slow and trying to tune into what they want.

# IF YOU HURT SOMEONE

If you are the person who hurt someone, it's time to listen to what they want. Often they will want some space and time away from you. After some time they might want you to listen to them, or to someone else on their behalf, about what you did. They might also want you to take responsibility and say what you are going to do to show that you have learned from it and won't do it again.

# Chapter Nine

# Consent in groups

A lot of the time you're doing stuff, you're going to be in a group of people.

It could be a group of friends, hanging out with family, being in class, at a youth group, playing sports, playing in a band, or something else. So how do you do consent when there are several people to consider?

Most of what I've covered so far is relevant to group situations, too. It's important that in these situations we are trying to maximize consent for everyone as much as possible. Obviously where there are more people then there are going to be lots of different needs, so finding one way of doing something that will please everyone is going to be difficult. Again, there is a trade-off going on. You might not be able to choose the exact thing you want, so you compromise, but this is because you think it will be a greater reward for doing something in a group. Joining your individual agency with other people leads to collective agency. Collective agency can not only be more fun, but you can also achieve more.

## GOING TO THE MOVIES WITH FRIENDS

Say your best friends are organizing going to see a movie together. You really want to see *2 Thin, 2 Crispy* but they all really want to see *Pepperoni Wars* (insert your own favorite movies here). You're like a +4 about *Pepperoni Wars* and they are all +8 or +9 about it. Maybe you'll go along anyway because you value being with them and you know that the experience of watching it together will be fun. And hey, maybe you'll like it. There's also the added benefit of being able to say, "I told you so" over a milkshake afterward when *Pepperoni Wars* turns out to be too long and kinda boring.

Perhaps you could say all of this to your friends and they'd say, "Are you sure?" and you'd say, "Yeah and if it's terrible I'll say I told you so," and they'd say "Chill."

But what if you really don't want to see *Pepperoni Wars*? You could say to your friends, "Hey, I really don't want to go to see *Pepperoni Wars*. I'm actually like a -3 about it, so I'd be doing something I don't want to do if I came with you." Perhaps they could say, "Oh okay, thanks for letting us know. Let's think of some different options." You could split up and some of you watch *2 Thin, 2 Crispy* and the others watch *Pepperoni Wars*. You could then meet up afterward and talk about it.

It can be hard saying what we want in this situation because, as we've discussed, it's difficult to ask someone to meet our needs anyway. If there are a group of people, it can be even more tricky because we might not want to feel like we are letting everyone else down. Also, because there are more people around, it might feel a little bit riskier to ask for what you want if you're worried about what people think. In this situation, there can be a lot of pressure and it can be easy to feel like we have no choice. Remember that you are saying "no" to them and "yes" to you, and that's important.

If you're in a group, it's really important that you're aware of this dynamic because it can be really awful to feel like we don't have a choice. It's easy for people to feel left out in groups and that can

be very painful. So perhaps if you are a person in the group who feels confident to talk about it, you could help everyone out by starting the conversation. Put some of the stuff in this chapter into practice.

You could say things like, "So how are we all feeling about *Pepperoni Wars*?" Or you could ask everyone to go through the movies that are showing and give their rating from -10 to +10. Even once you are in the line, you could check that everyone is still feeling okay about the decision. Is everyone excited and enthusiastic, or are some people looking like they aren't that into the idea anymore? You could say, "Oh I noticed that *2 Thin, 2 Crispy* is on at the same time— if anyone wants to see that they could."

## TEAMWORK

There's a very special kind of love that we can get from feeling like we're part of a team. Having a sense of purpose and something that you all want to achieve together can far outweigh the compromises that you might have to put up with along the way. This is particularly true when you're doing something in a team because it's possible for everyone to have a specific role for a specific purpose.

If you play soccer (or any sport) you might have had a kick around with your friends that was just for fun and didn't matter how good you were. But in competitive soccer, you would all perform roles within the team so that you could all play more effectively. You could each take on the role that most suits your abilities. Playing in midfield is for those good at passing, a fast runner can play on the wing, and if you have very

large hands, you might be good in goal. Everyone could talk about this beforehand by looking at all the different roles and thinking about who might be happiest in each role.

In teams or groups, people can take different roles. There's often someone who has a leadership role, someone who mediates between different people, someone who comes up with ideas, and someone who takes action to get things done. This can happen in groups of people quite naturally because people can fit into these roles. So consent here is about dividing up tasks that will help each person in the team to have agency, and at the same time having agency as a team. Having both of those things together can feel really great, but only if you are able to have the kinds of consent conversations I've been talking about.

# CONSENT AND THE WORLD

Back when I was boring you about pizza, I said that not everyone has the same freedom to choose and I would come to that later in the book. Well, this is that bit! There are lots of reasons why some people find it easier to choose and ask for what they want. It's important that you know about this because everyone has different levels of freedom. Everyone has different amounts of agency.

This is where it's all a bit political but/and super important.

# Chapter Ten
# Gender

Men and women get very different messages about how to live, their agency, choices, and consent.

I really hope this changes soon because the idea that men and women are very different and should be treated differently has been around for hundreds of years. It's not true, and it's really, really bad. Also male and female aren't the only genders—there are lots of non-binary genders that many people identify with and that all need to be recognized.

"I am not free while any woman is unfree, even when her shackles are very different from my own"
-Audre Lorde

Anyway, the basic idea is that men are taught by society to be active, tough, carefree, and rational. On the other hand, women are taught by society that they should be whatever men are not. So they are meant to be passive, soft, caring, and emotional. If this sounds like another Should Story, then you're right. It's bad, right? It's basically saying that men have agency and women do not.

Feminist writers, teachers, and activists have been fighting this Should Story for hundreds of years. Nine hundred years ago, a writer called Hildegard of Bingen said that genders should be seen as different but equal. In the 1940s, Simone de Beauvoir wrote *The Second Sex*, which talked about how society is structured around men and masculinity.

Men get to be the heroes of their own stories, while women are the other characters, or the objects, in stories. It shocked people when the book came out over 70 years ago, but we still have a long way to go before women are treated equally.

Learning about feminism from writers like Simone de Beauvoir and Audre Lorde, another important feminist writer, has made lots of people want to raise their kids to be feminists, too. But even if we were taught differently about this stuff when we were growing up, we might find that the rest of the world doesn't think the same way. Think about how many movies and TV shows are pretty much all about men and compare that to how many are all about women. See what I mean?

"one is not born, but rather becomes, a woman" simone de Beauvoir

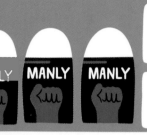

Gender, feminism, and sexism is a whole other book, but it's super important when it comes to consent, particularly if men and women want to do things together, which they do. It's very, very popular in fact.

If men are taught that they are supposed to be active, then they are supposed to make the decisions about what they want to do with someone else. If women are taught that they are supposed to be passive, then they have to wait for someone else to make the decisions for them. And when it comes to sex, there is often an extra level of difficulty. Think of words used to describe men who have lots of sex. Now think of words used to describe women who have lots of sex. Can you see how men get status for being interested

dainty dainty Delicate Delicate

GENTLE ♥♥  Ladylike

...ylike soft soft so...

meek meek meek mee...

in sex and women get shamed?

In a perfect world, this Should Story would mean that men learn more about how to do consent: like how to ask, how to give options, and how to listen to a "no." However, this sadly isn't the case for a lot of men, and many men either intentionally, or less intentionally, use their power to hurt and abuse women. Of course men can also be hurt by women and people of other genders, but if you look up the statistics, you'll see that many more women are forced to have sex than men.

Choosing a pizza is hard enough. Things like negotiating a greeting or having sex are harder. But the different messages that men and women get about freedom and agency make this even harder STILL. But there's more (sorry).

floral calm  flawless' flawless' flawless' flawless...

Silk Silk Silk Silk  coy coy coy

GENDER

airy airy fr... fr... fr...

# Chapter Eleven

# How "isms" make consent harder

We've talked about sexism and how that can make it quite difficult when men and women want to do things together.

Sexism gives women less agency and less freedom. This is also true of other "isms." Next, we'll talk about just a few of these different kinds of "isms"—but there are many others. This shows that we have a long way to go to make the world a fairer and more equal place for everyone.

# RACISM

Racism means that people get less agency and freedom than other people because of their race. Many things in our world are designed by and for white people, restricting people of color and their freedom to choose. People of color are often treated less consensually by authorities than white people. For example, black and brown people are not as safe from harm, abuse, or harassment in public as white people are.

# CLASSISM

Classism means that people with money and wealth have much more agency and power than people who don't. There are millions of people in the world who don't get to choose what pizza they want or what show to watch, because they don't have the financial opportunity to do either of those things.

# HOMO/BI/TRANSPHOBIA

There are also people's experiences of homophobia or biphobia: where people who like people of the same gender are told that it's going to be really hard for them to find someone to love. Transphobia means that many people who are trans (they don't identify with the gender assigned to them at birth) often face violence and discrimination.

# ABLEISM

Disabled people are often treated as if they
aren't going to be able to take part in society
on the same level as people who aren't disabled.
But that's because we have created a society
that works better for abled people and
gives them more freedom and choice
than disabled people.

What we all need to do is to smash sexism, racism, classism, homo/bi/transphobia, and ableism. So let's go and make steps to do that. While we do, we also have to remember that we don't all have the same benefits, opportunities, and freedoms because some of us live in crappy societies and communities that deny those things to people because of who they are.

So when you're having consent conversations, remember that one person may well have more freedom to make their choices than others. People's experiences of stigma and shame can make it more difficult for them to ask for what they want. Also remember that many people experience more than one of these "isms" at a time (the word for this is intersectionality, which was first used by a feminist called Kimberlé Crenshaw). For example, a man might have more power to choose because he is a man, but also less if he is a disabled man.

Obviously, when we're having consent conversations we are talking to individuals—remember Margey... and Rita. (You got that this is a pizza joke, right? Margherita? Oh, forget it.) Individuals will each have their own experiences and stories about how they navigate "isms" that they face. If someone has been called names, stared at, or threatened in public, just for being who they are, then that might affect how confident they feel in going out in certain places and at certain times, for instance.

As well as identity, people's experiences can also affect how they feel about themselves. Things from our childhood can have an effect on whether we feel able to choose, such as neglect, bullying, or being told bad things, such as that we're unattractive, we're not allowed to be soft, or we can't ask for things.

ISM

S SISM

S SEXISM

BI-TRANS-

OBIA

ACISM

# DIFFERENCES IN POWER

So if one person has grown up with less choice because of their identity or their experiences, what happens if they meet someone who has more choice? How can people choose a pizza, what show to watch, or how to greet each other if one person has more choices available to them than another?

Here are some examples (that I've made up). Two are about sex, so I'm sounding the sex alarm again. Skip over those if you like.

I've been friends with someone for about a year and I think I like them. I don't feel very attractive and everyone likes her. She also has a lot more friends than I do, so I worry if I tell her that I would lose the friendship.

I know that I have all the good games, so when he comes over I like to try and give him more choice about what he wants to play. I'm careful not to be patronizing about it, but I think that I'm being a good friend if I give options. He always looks out for me at school and makes me feel included with all his friends, so it's definitely a two-way thing.

WE HAVE THIS REALLY CLOSE FRIENDSHIP. KINDA LIKE A BROMANCE, RIGHT? I USED TO GET BULLIED A LOT AND FOUND IT DIFFICULT TO TRUST PEOPLE. HE'S NEVER HAD THAT KIND OF PROBLEM BUT HAS ALWAYS BEEN REALLY KIND TO ME. I CAN'T TALK TO ANYONE LIKE I CAN TALK TO HIM. HE'S INTRODUCED ME TO SO MANY GREAT EXPERIENCES AND THINGS—LIKE BANDS, MOVIES, AND ALL HIS FRIENDS—AND I ALWAYS GO ALONG WITH IT. I WORRY THAT HE'S GOING TO FIND OTHER FRIENDS BECAUSE HE THINKS I'M BORING AND THAT I BRING NOTHING TO THE PARTY.

They all come from families who have more money than I do, so sometimes I miss out on doing things with them. That means that I often feel left out when they talk about things they've done together that I wasn't able to do. So sometimes I feel like I can't take part in the group.

MY PARTNER IS REALLY HOT. THEY ARE SUPER CONFIDENT ABOUT WHAT THEY WANT FROM SEX AND I GO ALONG WITH IT. IT'S OKAY I GUESS, BUT IT'S NOT REALLY DOING IT FOR ME AND I'M NOT SURE HOW I CAN BRING IT UP.

My disabilities mean that I have to talk about my needs a lot with people. It's something that I've learned how to do over the years and so now I'm quite confident about it. I've done that with my friends and now they are all much better at trying to meet my needs. They just really get it, you know? They ask other people about their needs now too, which is great. It means I've taught them about how to empower disabled people.

*We have such a great time together. At first he kept asking what I liked, which I found a bit tricky. But we've built up so much trust together that he's made it easier for me to say what I like without making me feel ashamed. It's tricky when you're a woman because if you admit you like sex you're seen as slutty. I never feel that way with him.*

If you think about the relationships you've had with people, maybe you've had a similar experience. Can you think of anything that the other person could have done to make the situation easier? Have you been on the other side of any of these situations yourself, with more agency and freedom than someone else you know? How have you handled it? When one person has more freedom and agency than another, they have more power. That creates a difference in power in their relationship. But it might not be obvious when it's happening. So this is why it's important that we're all aware of consent all of the time, and not just when we are thinking about sex. We need to maximize each other's freedom and agency. That means we need to do more asking, more listening, give more options, give people space, notice what is going on for the other person, and sometimes just not do the thing you want to do.

Chapter Twelve

# Empower each other with consent

As Toni Morrison, a writer and activist, once said,
"I tell my students, 'When you get these jobs that you have been so brilliantly trained for, just remember that your real job is that if you are free, you need to free somebody else. If you have some power, then your job is to empower somebody else. This is not just a grab-bag candy game.'"

You can see that consent isn't just something that is about us and our relationships with other people. It's also about the world, and the structures that we live in.

# How can we use our choices, freedoms, agency, and power to allow others to have the same choices, freedoms, agency, and power?

What can we do in our schools, our neighborhood, our circle of friends, and our family? How can we use our collective agency to make the world fairer, more just, and more equal?

This is where activism and politics are really important. It's why people get involved in campaigns like **#MeToo**, **#BlackLivesMatter**, and disability rights. It's why people ask their schools to do better when educating students about relationships and sex. It's why people go on strike for climate change. But it's also important to do these things consensually, by asking people what they want and need, offering the help we can, and having ongoing conversations about how to work together.

We can all make a start by trying to do more consent on a daily basis with each other and about everything. Learning to give ourselves and each other the most amount of choices, freedoms, agency, and power as we can. It's not always easy, but it's always important, so I think we should always try. That's one Should Story I can get behind.

# Activities

In this section, there are
some activities to help you
take what you've learned
about consent out
into the world.

# HOW TO BUY A...

As well as pizza, I spend a lot of time thinking about what chocolate bar I want. Sometimes I just grab the first one I see and pick the wrong thing. So here are some questions to help us both to decide what chocolate bar to get next time. If you don't like chocolate you could go with chips, soda or fruit (lol, just kidding).

How much do you want to spend?

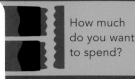

TOFFEE

TOFFEE

COCONUT

SALTY
SALTY
SALTY

How big do you want the chocolate bar to be?

MILK
MILK
MILK
MILK

How chocolate-y do you want it to be (all chocolate, some chocolate, or a little chocolate)?

 Do you want to try something totally new? Or do you want something you know you like, or something you haven't had in a while?

ALMOND  MOND  MOND

Do you want the whole chocolate bar to be super sweet or a bit more bitter?

Do you want some other flavors too? Like caramel, fruit, raisins (that's a fruit), nuts, cookie, or nougat?

LEMON
LEMON
LEMON

Do you want white, milk, or dark chocolate?

DAR
DAR
DAR

WHITE
WHITE

CRUMBLE
CRUMBLE
CRUMBLE

COOKIES  IES

FRUITY
FRUITY
FRUITY

# CHOCOLATE BAR

Think about the texture. Light and airy? Crumbly? Crunchy? Chewy? Or do you want a solid, chunky bite of chocolate?

If you get some serious FOMO, just gently remind yourself that it's okay if you don't get it totally right this time around. There's always next time.

If you're really struggling to work out what you want, you could think about what you definitely don't want. If you spend a bit of time thinking about what chocolate you definitely don't want, then that can help you to think about the kinds of things that you do want in a chocolate bar.

Then when you eat it, really pay attention to how it tastes and make some notes.

# CHOOSE WHAT TO WATCH

Think back to chapter 3, when we looked at how to choose what to watch with someone. Here's a guide to help you next time!

 Comforting

 Thought-provoking

 Excited

### What do you want to watch?

 TV

 Movie

### Which subjects interest you?

 Drama

 Thriller

 Comedy

 Scary

 Real-life story

### What kind of mood do you want to be in?

 Silly

 Serious

 Relaxing

Romantic story

**Do you want to watch something you've:**

 Seen before

 Something new

**How do you want to watch it?**

 Just on in the background

 Watch it but talk to each other

 Mostly watch it but it's okay to check phones

 Watch it seriously

 Don't take it seriously and laugh at it

**You can use this system to tell each other how you feel about different options:**

● Red (things that would be a trigger for you or something you have a phobia about)

● Amber (things that are tricky for you to watch but you'd be okay)

● Green (things you would be totally fine to watch)

**How do you check in with each other about whether you still want to watch it?**

 Making time to pause it

 Checking each time you pause to go to the bathroom

 Agree to watch the whole thing (so long as it's not Red for you)

# YOUR LAST

Think about your last five greetings that you had with someone. For each one, note down:

## Who was involved?

## What kind of greeting was it?

## How good was it?

-10 --------- 0 ---------- +10

Terrible    Meh    Amazing

## Did you have the greeting you wanted or was it more the greeting they wanted?

Their ideal greeting

Mutually good and nice

Your ideal greeting

# FIVE GREETINGS

**Was your greeting:**

A Should Story greeting

A heavily negotiated greeting

A slow greeting where attention
was carefully paid to what we
both wanted

**What made it harder or easier for you to
have the greeting you wanted?**

Equal power / unequal power

Awkward / relaxed

Not enough time / loads of time

I wasn't confident / I was very confident

They were patient / they weren't patient

**Note down what you have learned about how to
improve your next greetings.**

**Think about what other people could do to make your
greetings better. What do you wish you could teach
them or ask them?**

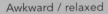
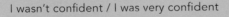
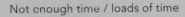

# WHO GETS AGENCY?

In the last couple of chapters, we explored how different identities can affect consent. This activity will help you to understand this in a bit more detail. Try creating six different characters, ideally a mix of different kinds of people with different identities.

You can draw them if you want, even as stick characters. You could also pick six characters from a TV show that you know really well, like *Game of Thrones*, *Friends*, *Brooklyn Nine-Nine*, or *Fresh Prince*. Or use your imagination, which is probably more fun.

You could use these drawings as a basis for your characters if you wanted.

Here are some things to think about when creating your character:

**Their name**

**Their gender**

**How they like to look**

**Their age**

**What they do**

**Their race**

**Any disabilities**

**Their class background**

**Religious beliefs**

**How much money they have**

**Their sexuality**

**Their friends**

**Their hobbies**

**Five words to describe them**

Try to have an idea of their back story too. What was life like for them at home, at school, or in their community? Were they treated well by the people around them? How fairly were they treated? What was expected of them? How do they feel about their body?

Now think about some of the things we have discovered in the book. Which characters might feel quite confident asking for what they want? Are there any pairings where one person might find it difficult to ask for what they want? Who gets to eat whatever pizza they like?

# GLOSSARY

**Ableism** Because we have created a society that does not work as well for people who are disabled, abled people have more freedom and choice than disabled people.

**Agency** The power to make decisions for ourselves.

**Asexuality** An identity that indicates that people experience no or little sexual attraction or desire. Also known as "ace."

**Asking** Where we invite others to do something for us, for them, or for each other.

**Biphobia** Where bi people (bisexual or biromantic) are given less agency and freedom than straight people because of their sexuality. This also includes being bullied, harassed, or attacked just for being bi.

**Choices** The various different options we might have when making a decision. It's always good to be given more choices, but sometimes having too many choices can be a bit much. It's okay to choose not to choose sometimes (so long as that's our choice).

**Collective agency** Where we join our individual agency with other people so that we can all do something together that is good, fun, or interesting.

**Consent** Being free to choose to agree to do something, with someone else, in groups, in the world and with yourself.

**Feminism** The fight against sexist Should Stories. Famous feminists include: Hildegard of Bingen, Simone de Beauvoir, and Audre Lorde.

**FOMO** Fear of missing out. This is sometimes used as a form of peer pressure to make you do something rather than not doing something.

**Freedom** The ability to do whatever we want, without preventing other people doing what they want.

**Greetings** What happens when we meet each other. Things like handshakes, fist bumps, and salutes.

**Homophobia** Where gay or lesbian people are given less agency and freedom than straight people because of their sexuality. This also includes being bullied, harassed, or attacked just for being gay or lesbian.

**"Isms"** Also known as "oppressions." Where some people are given less agency than non-oppressed people because of their identity. This includes things such as ableism, racism, and sexism.

**Maybe** Somewhere between "yes" and "no". It's okay to be "maybe." Perhaps you need more time, information, or ideas on how you could do the thing. Or not.

**Men** The Should Story about men is that they are meant to be active, hard, carefree, and rational. The Should Story says that men are supposed to be like this and women and other genders are not allowed to be like this. It's bad for everyone.

**Mushrooms** A fungus that is on a lot of pizzas. Why?

**No** If someone says no, it means they don't want to do something. There are lots of ways to say "no," even without saying anything. So even if someone doesn't use the word no, they could still be giving you a "no."

**Non-binary gender** A gender identity that isn't "man" or "woman," such as genderqueer, hijra, or two-spirit.

**Noticing** Using all of your available senses to figure out whether you or someone else wants to do something. It's about slowing down and paying attention to yourself, other people and the Should Stories.

**Pizza** Thin bread cooked in an oven with sauce and toppings (mmmmm... pizza).

**Politics** How we can join all of our agencies together to make the world more consensual and more equal for everyone.

**Power** Because of unequal societies, some people get more freedom to choose than others. This gives some people more power than others. If we have more power over someone, we need to be better at consent with them.

**Racism** Where people of color get less agency and freedom than white people because of their race. This means not being treated fairly and having to face violence and discrimination because of their race.

**Self-care** Looking after yourself in a way that works best for you. How you can use your own agency to treat yourself consensually.

**Sex** Any activity by yourself or with someone else that you intend to cause sexual excitement. There's a Should Story about what counts as sex, but sex is many, many different things.

**Sexism** Where women get less agency and freedom than men because they are women. This includes the freedom to feel safe, equally valued, and respected.

**Should Story** A story that we tell ourselves (and is told to us) about what we should be doing. It's not about what is right or ethical, but more to do with what is "normal," like not putting strawberries on a pizza, or wearing mismatching socks.

***2 Thin, 2 Crispy*** A movie featuring a pizza chef/action hero. (Best joke in the book, IMHO.)

**Trans** Anyone whose gender identity doesn't match the one that was assigned to them at birth. This can include trans women, trans men, and non-binary people.

**Transphobia** Where trans people are given less agency and freedom than cis people (people whose gender identities match the one assigned at birth). This also includes being bullied, harassed or attacked just for being trans.

**Women** The Should Story for women is that they are supposed to be the opposite of men: passive, soft, caring, and emotional. It's sexist and wrong, and bad for both women and men, particularly when we talk about consent and agency.

**Yes** When someone wants to do something. If you want to be sure that someone really wants to do something, then give more than just the option of yes or no. Yes, no, or maybe. Or yes or no to different possible choices.

# RESOURCES

## ONLINE ADVICE AND INFORMATION

**BISH**—Okay, this one's mine. I write for over 14s about "sex, relationships, and you." As you can imagine, a lot of it's about consent and also about how to look after yourself. If you have a question about sex and relationships I've probably answered it there. It's mostly aimed at a UK audience but it's also popular in the US, so check it out!
**bishuk.com**

**Scarleteen**—this is an excellent sexuality and relationships advice website for young people. As well as lots of articles, they also have moderated forums where you can get help and advice.
**scarleteen.com**

**Sex Etc**—this is sex education and advice written by teens, for teens.
**sexetc.org**

## SERVICES IN REAL LIFE

There are lots of services in real life that you can access if you need anything to do with sexual health, sexual violence, or abuse. Search for "sexual health services" or "sexual healthcare," or "medical centre."

You could speak to a trusted and wise adult to try to find a service for you. Try to look for services that say they are confidential and private. Ideally, they would also be free or at least low cost. Try to make sure that they are unbiased and will let you make your own decisions. It's okay for you to take someone along with you to help support you—perhaps by asking questions for you, or making sure you have the information you need.

All services should be good at consent. So they should give you options, give you information about what happens, and should always give you the option of saying "no." If you get the vibe that they aren't good at consent, it's always okay for you to leave and try to find someone else. If you find a good service, let me know on social media **@bishsexed** on Twitter and Instagram and I will share them.

You can also report sexual assault or violence to the police, who should also be able to find support for you. If you are in immediate danger, call 911 to access police services.

## SEE ALSO

**Planned Parenthood**—They provide sexual health services across the US. These are either low cost or free to young people in some places.
**plannedparenthood.org**

**RAINN**—This is the largest anti-sexual violence organisation in the US. They also run the National Sexual Assault Hotline which you can call. It's a safe and confidential helpline that is available 24/7. They have trained staff members who can support you and who can put you in touch with a local sexual assault service provider.
Website: **rainn.org/get-help**
Hotline: 800.656.HOPE (4673)

# ACKNOWLEDGMENTS

## FROM JUSTIN

Firstly, a huge thank you to all the young people I've worked with in real life about consent. I know the Should Story is that you are meant to learn from me, but I've also learned a lot from you. Your insights have helped my thinking about consent, and a lot of it is in this book. Big thanks to everyone who supports my work at BISH. You're helping me help thousands of young people every day. Massive love to my mate and colleague Meg-John Barker. I've learnt tons from you in our work on consent, relationships, love, politics, and sex. Thanks for reading this and for supporting me. Thanks to Dr Eleanor Janega for reading the manuscript and for your support. Also huge thanks to my friends and family who have been encouraging of my interesting, and at times challenging, career. A huge thanks to everyone at Frances Lincoln for asking me to write this book. Thanks to Claire Grace and Lucy Menzies for being so supportive, patient, and wise with your edits. Thank you to Karissa for your amazing design work. And finally, thanks to Fuchsia MacAree, your illustrations are absolutely stunning. They made me giggle a lot and cry a little bit!

## FROM FUCHSIA

Thanks to Justin for writing such an engaging, fun, and informative book. It's been a delight to bring the words to life! As always, gratitude to Sal O'Halloran and Ruan van Vliet for their ideas and help throughout this (and especially for when Ruan came up with the perfect solution for a drawing before I had even told him what it was about). To Ciarán, thanks for being kind and supportive always. And to the friends I snuck into this book who I haven't yet mentioned: Rob, Stina, Danny, Conor, Isadora, and Anna—find yourselves! Finally, thanks Karissa for being a dream to work with, and to Claire for getting me involved in this worthwhile and lovely project.

Inspiring | Educating | Creating | Entertaining

Brimming with creative inspiration, how-to projects, and useful information to enrich your everyday life, Quarto Knows is a favorite destination for those pursuing their interests and passions. Visit our site and dig deeper with our books into your area of interest: Quarto Creates, Quarto Cooks, Quarto Homes, Quarto Lives, Quarto Drives, Quarto Explores, Quarto Gifts or Quarto Kids.

Text © 2021 Justin Hancock. Illustrations © 2021 Fuchsia MacAree.

First published in 2021 by Frances Lincoln Children's Books, an imprint of The Quarto Group.
100 Cummings Center, Suite 265D, Beverly, MA 01915, USA.
T +1 978-282-9590 F +1 078-283-2742 **www.QuartoKnows.com**

A catalog record for this book is available from the British Library.

ISBN 978-0-7112-5656-9

The illustrations were created digitally.
Set in Avenir, Belwe Mono, Column

Published by Katie Cotton and Georgia Amson-Bradshaw
Designed by Karissa Santos
Commissioned by Claire Grace
Edited by Claire Grace and Lucy Menzies
Production by Dawn Cameron

Manufactured in Guangdong, China TT102020

10 9 8 7 6 5 4 3 2 1

MIX
Paper from
responsible sources
FSC® C016973